Be The Light of the World

John Davis

Original Cover Art by Nancy Davis
Editing by Phyllis Miner and Alan Tutt
Layout by Alan Tutt

ISBN-10: 1542596009
ISBN-13: 9781542596008

Additional copies may be purchased at Amazon.com.

Foreword

Universal love and world unity are the two instruments to heal the wounds of a planet starving for wisdom, and fervently praying for a permanent world peace.

In this book, we will explore the power of the Word and of thoughts as tools of manifestation.

Each of us is a co-creator with the Supreme Creator, whether we realize it or not. We create for good or ill by the nature of our thoughts, words, and deeds. Every person has the capacity to change the world. All it takes is intentional effort to manifest the world we desire.

If each of us, with proper intent and motivation, takes responsibility for the nature of quality of our thoughts and the proper care of the little piece of Earth over which we have stewardship, we could eliminate the negativity, fear, and degradation that presently exist on the planet. If each of us chooses to care for our fellow human beings who are less fortunate than ourselves, in a spirit of philanthropy, we could eliminate suffering and want among the human family. These are realistic and achievable goals.

A simple daily regimen of meditation, prayer, and practical action in whatever form suits you—volunteerism, environmental activism, or other humanitarian endeavor—is all that is required to recreate the world. It does require discipline and the willingness to encourage others to do the same, for manifestation works best when the participants are great in number.

This is a calling, which the World Server hears. Every person on the planet who responds to the inner desire to serve in some fashion is a part of this group of world servers, and the contribution of each is as significant as that of the collective.

Many prophecies have been made regarding our planet's birthing into the Great Age of Enlightenment. The predictions of two prophets, Nostradamus and Edgar Cayce, have been thoroughly documented in their books and readings. In many minds, the biblical book of Revelations has laid down forecasts of things to manifest in the coming age.

Our world is presently closing out two major cycles at the same time: the change of one century into another, and the close of a 2600-year age (from Piscean to Aquarian). Only once before have these conditions existed on planet Earth, and this was prior to written records being kept—over 8,000 years before Christ. Now, the same patterns of completion and new birth are occurring all at the same time.

On March 21, 2012, I decided to write this book, exactly nine months before the Mayan Prophecy regarding December 21, 2012. The Coptic Fellowship met on that day at our National Headquarters in Grand Rapids, Michigan to create a planetary group mental seed for the magnificent, positive birth of this famous Mayan Prophecy.

There were multiple degrees of expectancy, ranging from "the greatest day ever" to "the end of the world." In my work as a planetary numerologist, I knew the scientific interpretation of this date to be "The Light of the World."

I realized that a book had to be written to prepare every person who was ready to actually become the Light of the World to fulfill their Aquarian destiny by becoming a co-creator to create a much more positive earth plane with permanent world peace and the greatest economy the souls on Earth have ever realized.

About the Author

John Davis is Director of the Coptic Fellowship International, an action-oriented modern philosophy based upon laws of balanced living originally introduced by the Egyptian Mystery Schools. He is also Director of the Spiritual Unity of Nations, dedicated to "The World as One Family," and Founder of the World Service Order program, training metaphysical leaders since 1985.

John is an Egyptologist who has taken 30 tours to Egypt, and an internationally-known personal and planetary numerologist who has given over 13,000 numerology readings.

Other Books by John Davis

Messiah and the Second Coming (1981)
Revelation for Our Time (1997)

Websites for More Information

TheKeysToYourDestiny.com

TheCopticCenter.org

SpiritualUnityofNations.org

Table of Contents

Section 1:
Let there be light!

We Desperately Need More Light

"It was the best of times, it was the worst of times ..." Charles Dickens wrote this in 1859, yet it applies today more so than ever. Our world is in chaos, with terrorism and war closer to our doorstep than any other time in history. Yet, we have progressed in other ways that could never have been imagined in those simpler times.

Scientific achievement and development of communications have changed the way we relate to others tremendously. Both avenues have created new interests and new groups. Values of long standing have dramatically changed. The old mores seem to be outdated. People are no longer isolated in total aloneness. Technological discoveries have brought our neighbors to our door. We are globally aware of the problems that confront our neighbors on the extreme side of the planet. We know when our brothers and sisters are hungry and hurting.

With this technological explosion has come the outstanding possibility of eliminating the major causes of hunger and alienation of humankind. Agriculture development and industrial techniques have given the world a new horizon of hope. Economic problems could be the simplest to solve if government, industry, and science share openly their visions and resources on a common grassroots level.

On national levels, it demands common sense, selflessness on national scales, freedom from political self-interests and an overall urgency for groups and nations to altruistically give their bounty in all areas of common endeavors.

Because of the expansion of communication, information has spread rapidly around the globe. The anxiety created by negative subliminal influences has brought peoples together for purposes of exploring ways of self-protection.

Recognizing their responsibilities and an ability to do something about the proliferation of the instruments of destruction, we have found a solution. We have become involved in the process of planetary transformation, dedicated to achieving the power of the Light of the World by personal purification and protection of light in our lives.

We Are All Connected

Many great civilizations had existed upon the Earth in times past, developed by masterful beings. But civilizations rose and fell as citizens interpreted the Word as they saw fit.

Finally the memory of their God grew dim.

Now we are at the threshold of another New Day, and spiritual power—latent in humankind—is spreading throughout the highways and byways of the planet.

Science has given impetus to the spreading of "The Word." Modern communication systems have given the Word wings, allowing it to reach the far and desolate regions of the corners of the globe, as never before known in the last centuries of humanity's existence on Earth. The message has gone out to be picked up in remote mountains and valleys, the deserts and plains, wherever people dwell.

Truth is marching, walking, flying unto the corners of the globe so that no individual shall be without the hearing of it. The truth of 2,000 years ago is ringing out through the glorious bells of the new day. All shall hear the call and gather together to listen to the old, yet ever new sound, from the many world disciples of universality.

And yet, the news media in all forms has given the stance of portraying the spectacular and the dramatic. This is almost as threatening as a deliberate distortion of information. Free nations and government-controlled news seem to suffer the same potential ills. A truly free and independent, positive-inspired news media can promote good will and understanding among groups and nations, small and large, influencing the seed thoughts of young adults.

It's Time to Wake Up

Thinkers of the world have determined they must not be blind followers of any particular ideology or religious dogma.

The status of human affairs cannot be separated from spiritual reality and the altruistic giving of self. Intelligent learners know they cannot leave it "up to God." People must leave their spectator position and must become actively involved in productive avenues of life, and encourage their neighbors to commit their daily lives to par-excellence.

Will the world's peoples have the patience and endurance to go through a period of adjustment, giving way to what is best for the general good of all even if it means possibly sacrificing some personal resources for the benefit of the whole? Sacrifice has never been a popular concept but there are few alternatives left for accomplishing unity. Priorities have to be made. Values have to be examined. The haves must learn to share with the have-nots. This message has been said in many ways by many people for many years for the preparation for each of us becoming the Light of the World.

When humanity reaches the end of their own capacity to solve collective problems, they ultimately turn to the greater powers within for answers.

While science has made tremendous strides in its discoveries, these advancements have exacted a great price. While the benefits have been many, we all know the cost of the discovery of nuclear power.

Nuclear power has not given us so much a sense of awe, but of futility. This is where humankind has been for the past forty years.

How far do the minds of scientific researchers actually reach?

Scientific research is limited in that it is still conducted by humans with finite wisdom. A merging of spirituality and science could help alleviate the inadequacies of a purely scientific approach, and is, in fact, closer to reality today than ever before.

Physicists are discovering the very truths that eastern mystics have espoused for thousands of years. They are offering theories of a holographic nature to the universe, the probability of parallel universes, and of the power of thought to affect the outcome of scientific experiments. Scientists are discovering that the Source of life is not found in a test tube, but in higher, divine law.

The question of religion and science merging is a possibility. This is the question being asked of scientists and by them. Science and religion are meeting on common ground, exploring and testing each other, but for the most part, attempting to cooperate toward an equalized, sharing perspective.

The Age of Aquarius

We are witnessing the death pangs of the dying order of Pisces and the beginning of an enlightened civilization, the new Age of Aquarius. This is a time period of approximately 2,160 to 2,250 years in each cycle, of which there are 12 cycles.

The whole solar system is moving from one energy force field to another, and what we are witnessing today are the first shafts of light as it breaks upon the horizon of the human mind, awakening humanity to the realization of its own essential divinity, that the individual soul is in a process of becoming God realized.

Attaining conscious immortality has always been the great calling and responsibility of the great role of World Teacher known to Christians as Christ, elsewhere as Krishna, among the Buddhists as the Lord Maitreya, and among the Muslims as Muhammad. These names or titles or personifications are the great Light of the World, being one ultimate source.

It is not limited to any individual, nation, people, or tradition. The quicker each person realizes that he or she is a citizen of the planet, and destined to be a citizen of the universe, the sooner we will experience planetary transformation into higher awareness.

That awareness is multidimensional and one must learn to develop higher dimensions of being—attaining absolute freedom and heightened consciousness. This great vision—this divine realization—which is all part and parcel of the great events belonging to this new Aquarian Age, when the Great Light Bringers—the regents of the planet—will externalize their presence in diverse ways.

The Aquarian Age, whose symbol is the pouring of the "Waters of Life" upon humankind, has aroused in the individual a need for group consciousness and the inherent need to be of service to others.

Even though a person may still be temporarily burdened by old habits, creeds, and beliefs of long standing; traditional ways of thinking and acting; as well as superstitions ingrained from the past; the human is dramatically bursting from its binding cocoon.

Humanity wants to spread their global interest. They yearn to set their souls free and explore dimensions of truth not previously investigated or previously even contemplated. This is making them adventurous seekers into the realm of spirit and they like what they are feeling.

They test the forces of the universe, knowing truth is not beyond their reach, discovering facets of the human spirit unknown just a few short years ago. "Life" is now a love energy to be understood, expanded, shared, and enjoyed.

The Return to Universality

During this planetary transition, there is an increasing awareness that the Age of Separateness is starting to come to an end. There is a growing recognition of global interdependence—that we are, in actuality One humanity, One world, One true expression of divinity, One within the Godhead. This example of Universal Unity, no matter what each world religion calls this essence, can be best understood and practiced by truly understanding that our lives express through only One Center of Consciousness, even though many diversities outwardly exist.

There is a new vibration moving through the minds of young and old alike. They are starting to perceive a new alternative that any type of war, or personal accumulation of material possessions, is not the solution to complex world problems. It is the quiet reflection of a peaceful heart and a dedication to the international welfare of humanity that truly brings about a new order.

Fundamental values and precious freedoms are beginning to make sense. The awakening to personal responsibility is one of the first signs of true spiritual progress. This discovery is being made in congregations of youth all over the world. It is the person, the individual discovery of human dignity and self-worth, preservation and sharing of Earth's natural resources, and the unfolding of one's spiritual potential moving into strong group solidarity. It must ultimately establish a group mind set of practicality and maturity that will bring about a new, progressive, positively motivated world.

You Can Make A Difference

Your being the Light of the World can make a major difference in the planetary shift during this century. If you're looking for a solution to the problems of the world today, I've got news for you. You're it!

The key is how much each of us are willing to dedicate ourselves to daily prayer (immaculate mental conception) to ensure a positive fulfillment of the plan described in this book.

Through the ages, this knowledge was lost from the mind of humanity so that they dwelled in separation from God. When the Christ manifested in the perfect body and mind of Jesus for the three years of His public mission, humanity again was using finite concepts to interpret the spiritual meaning of the Christ light-infused Jesus.

More words have been written and spoken about God than any other subject in history. Had humanity listened to their own inner light and sought their divinity within, there would not have been this need. Humanity would have fellowshipped with their source in complete trust and love and would have known what their individual and collective role was. No darkness would have existed upon the Earth. It is only God's benevolent love for creation that led Him to bring forth the Light of the World, humankind's own individual birthright, through individual perfected beings such as Jesus, Moses, and Buddha.

The need for unity is emerging in every land on the face of the Earth. It is growing in the regions of Africa, and in the ice fields of the northern sun. The energy of God is there. In every language now spoken upon the Earth, the Christ, Krishna, Muhammad, or Buddha is anchored in the hearts and heard in the voices of the children of God. The Light of the World is in the energy of these groups as individuals share their own birthing experience.

The Lights of the World are returning to re-establish the Word that has been lost in the last 2,000 years. The Bible talks of "the latter days," of the sun and moon being darkened, the stars that will fall, and that the Lights of the World will come with a host of angels that will sound their trumpets seated upon the clouds of glory.

These conditions will manifest, but only in a symbolic sense. The negative inference in the above passage is actually positive when interpreted by the secret language.

If we could see the glory prepared for us in God's Kingdom, we would never hesitate in total commitment to our growth. We would dedicate total effort to achieving oneness with Father-Mother God, the most glorious of all possible happenings.

Be the Light of the World   John Davis

The Power of One Individual

Here's a friend who shares the same thing we feel: Wayne Dyer.

"One individual who lives and vibrates to the energy of optimism and a willingness to be nonjudgmental of others will counterbalance the negativity of 90,000 people who calibrate at a lower, weakening level.

"One individual who lives and vibrates to the energy of pure love and reverence will counterbalance the negativity of 750,000 individuals who calibrate at the lower level weakening levels.

"One individual who lives and vibrates to the energy of illumination, bliss, and intimate peace, will counterbalance the negativity of 10,000,000 people who calibrate at the lower weakening levels.

"One individual who lives and vibrates to the energy of grace, pure spirit beyond the body, in a world of non-duality or complete oneness, will counterbalance the negativity of 70,000,000 people who calibrate at the lower weakening levels."

Signed: Wayne Dyer.

Recommended Light of the World Prayer

The following prayer is recommended for all Light Workers to use daily.

Almighty Mother-Father-God, I pray for healings on all levels—physical, mental, emotional, and spiritual—in all families, in all hospitals & health centers, in all doctors' offices, psychologists' offices, in AA meetings, in addiction counseling sessions, and everywhere else were healing is needed and desired.

I pray that all politicians choose peace in all circumstances. (Bring Ten Commandments to national and international expression.) I pray that all of humanity remember that all children worldwide are symbolically our children, and all people are our brothers and sisters. I pray that women everywhere are empowered and experience equality with men. (All men and women are created equal.) I pray that slavery is eliminated from planet Earth. I pray that governmental laws be for the benefit "of the people, by the people, and for the people." (The hungry find food, the homeless find homes, and the sick and injured are healed.) I pray that all nations share their nation's natural resources with their people and other nations.

I pray that all religious and spiritual leaders to pray daily for all good to manifest on Earth, and they continually seek the manifestation of the peaceful coexistence and cooperation of religions. I pray that businesses succeed in all nations. And as a result of national and international business successes, everyone everywhere find meaningful, creative, life-sustaining work. I pray that the worldwide economy becomes the most successful and stable in the history of the planet.

Key Ideas Revealed in this Book

1. There is a "Plan" delivered from God (Hierarchy) through spiritual beings to Earth for the advancement of Humanity.
2. The more of us that work on The Plan, the quicker it will manifest.
3. NOW is a critical time.
4. The reader has been led to this book, and is therefore called by higher forces to join the cause.

5. There have been many masters who have worked to bring The Plan to this point, which is nearly completed.

6. The details revealed in this book (including The Plan) come from the science of planetary numerology, and Coptic texts preserved through history to contain the pure Truth. The Christian Bible has gone through many revisions, and therefore contains only partial Truth.

7. Moses, Christ, Buddha, King Arthur, and Hamid Bey were all examples of people who responded to the call and attained mastery on Earth. If we follow their example, we will do well.

8. We work on The Plan through our thoughts, words, prayers, and deeds. Karmic Law (Cause & Effect) produces results based on the essence of what we do, say, and think.

9. We can all pray for world peace, and this is the first step in helping The Plan reach fulfillment.

10. Maintaining a positive focus will further influence Karmic Law to bring about peace on Earth.

11. Equality between the sexes is the most important change that needs to be made.

12. Spiritual Unity of Nations is an organization dedicated to helping individuals and organizations in their efforts to serve humanity.

13. The Coptic Fellowship exists to help individuals realize their Divine Potential.

Section 2:
Light, Glorious Light!

Lights of Love

Those who were here and came again,
And hereafter will be known
As humanity's best friend
Whose logo of a diamond
Comes from a rising sun
Means power that's pure for an Age begun.
Whose love for humanity
Shines so bright
No one can doubt their spiritual might.
The promise of these lights of the world
Is that all can rise
And none need fail.
And that which was wrought in a mountain glen
Is now manifesting
In the hearts of all humanity.

A gift from Clarence Zion

The Universe Anticipates

The power of the Almighty God is indeed a marvelous thing to see. The hills will ring forth. The heavens will resound with the vibration of their countenance. The Universe is already anticipating the approach of the world light. The sun will burst forth in glory, the stars will outshine the sun as they reflect the diamond brilliance of the Lights of the World.

The major influence of the emerging Aquarian Age is the awakening of humanity to its divinity and its place in the universe. This awakening has been referred to as the attainment of Christ Consciousness, but it has seeds in all traditions, for it results from the activity of light on human consciousness.

Alice Bailey described the development of the human being as "a succession of expansions" in awareness, where consciousness progresses from a personality-centered focus, to a higher-self or soul-centered focus, and then to a spirit-centered focus until it reaches divinity. This can be alternately described as "stages" of growth humanity is experiencing, and the evolution toward Christ Consciousness is presently in its second stage, to be fully realized with the establishment of the Spiritual Unity of Nations.

To dedicate one's energy to spiritual world unity does not mean one has to surrender one's own religious beliefs or philosophical affiliation. It does require transcending one's concepts to see the larger plan for unity, to carefully scrutinize the objectives of harmonious cooperation.

Jesus Himself often said, "And it is likened unto this," meaning it was impossible even for Him to determine how this great plan of unified vision would develop, but He provided many parables to illustrate His interpretation of its great potential of magnificence.

A Spiritual Vision

According to our principles at this time, and the overall observation of our planet, it is apparent there is a tremendous need for an overt change in consciousness—an overt change of thought and concentration. Within the pinnacle of the society of limitations, the way shown forth by us as humans must be through dramatic change in our form of confidence to extract that which we know to be true, beyond the shadow of what we call a reasonable doubt.

The New Age message is one of illumination, freedom, and joy, with a sense of wonder, and a glorious plan divine. Thank God the time has come for humanity to take the greatest stride of soul we have ever taken.

The challenge is an adventure into God. The great God power has broken through the great cloud of unknowing and has pierced through to the human brain, and is being released by mighty reverberations of energy and power.

We cannot continue to call upon souls to believe in blind faith. We ask them to seek anew the ancient, ageless, eternal truths of being. Their concept of God, Christ, spirit, and truth will change toward a greater cosmic awareness.

There can never be a real peace on Earth until humanity is united in its ideals and sense of purpose toward the goal of equality and freedom for all people without regard to gender, race, spiritual belief, or nationality.

Due to its inherent intent to promote the virtues of love and goodwill among people, the spiritual organization or religious institution is the logical vehicle by which its goal can be achieved. It was with this in mind that the Spiritual Unity of Nations was formed, an organization whose goal it is to create a body of leaders from all spiritual and peace-advocating traditions to promote and foster spiritual unity among all people in the pursuit of world peace.

People who are spiritually awake will be calling for unity in increasingly greater numbers. And they will not be doing so as a single mind, but with the wonderful diversity that characterizes humankind.

For it is not in creating identical entities that this great goal will be accomplished. The strength of our species is in its variety. Each tradition will work within its own system to promote peace through unity. These groups are like the rays of the sun, merely individual streams of light, but united, they radiate the awesome power of a star. This is the vision of the Spiritual Unity of Nations.

The Great Age Has Started

The Great Age has started! The unification of souls is the challenge of the day! A universal vision, we must awake to it!

There is a stirring and awakening in the innermost hearts and minds of individuals all over the world, but they are waiting for guidance. They are waiting for a message, they are waiting for messengers.

The messenger in this case is multiple. Many voices, but one message—the spiritual unity of humanity!

The old order dictating, "I am right and you are wrong," is dying. Be pro the truth! No place exists in our thinking and planning to anything that is anti. It's all been tried before and achieved very little. Be pro the truth, pro the light, pro the God presence, and be as positive and as direct, as informative as possible!

Know ye not ye are the Light of the World? Isn't that positive? We always have been and still are the children of Light!

We have to bring a degree of light to those who walk in darkness and in shadows and various shades of gray. They will sense the universality of our message.

We should go forth, start anew and lay foundations for current need. Lay foundations that will enable us to move forward under the light of our First Master, our soul, and rejoice in our own inner awakening, for where there is an awakening, there is a new sense of freedom! There can be no heaven without freedom! Freedom is of the spirit. All else binds.

So we must have a unity with a promise of freedom, not a uniformity. Uniformity would be chaos. It must be a freedom of a nature that will enable thirsty souls to sense heaven here and now that we are free and liberated souls not bound by anything or anyone of the past.

Now is the appointed hour!

The Future World

The future world will be one where fear will no longer be a tool for manipulation and control. Rather, children will grow up in a world with an understanding of the inherent goodness in a peace-loving people and where creativity is nurtured and love is the guiding principle.

Over the past couple of centuries or so, a trend has emerged toward a partnership model and away from the dominator model. This trend is evidenced in the various movements for social justice and equality, which can be viewed as steps in humanity's evolutionary quest for survival.

Among these movements is the founding of a nation on the edge of a pristine wilderness where people would experience true religious and civil freedom, a nation which was forged by men who held a higher ideal than the pursuit of dominance and power. The societal model for the future exists in the democratic ideal established during the latter part of the 18th century in the western hemisphere on the North American continent, an ideal which has its roots in the sacred traditions of our ancient forbears.

The New Age of Consciousness has to be a scientific age. It has to focus on a spiritual science that is going to win and save and inspire and guide the youth of the world. This must also include a higher mental nature, less devotional, carrying the best of the devotional qualities of the past ages and giving humanity a vision, an impulse, a new sense of direction symbolized in the concept of the spiritual unity of nations.

It was the great Christ who said, "Now is the appointed time." Not yesterday, not tomorrow, not in 10,000 years.

Time in the consciousness of the divine is always now. In the sense of nowness, we achieve a sense of oneness—oneness with the Christ, oneness with Hierarchy, oneness with the Great Light.

So it's the merging of mind with the Great Light that ultimately counts. We will become the Light of the World.

The realignment of the planets in recent time will still have some effect on humanity, depending on individual collective expressions of love.

If enough of us—as we are registering those frequencies—begin to work with extreme constructive effort, then the alignment will have a positive effect to the degree it will change the input, or the basic consciousness of thought, eradicating all of the unnecessary negative thought patterns. This happens on the fundamental level of thought, including the impetus and duration of vibrational frequencies, electromagnetic fields, atomic structure, as well as nuclear and biological chemistry.

These planetary alignment energies will then push those misguided thoughts out, smother, and dissipate them into the atomic structure, and then transmute them into an advanced formation. The breaking down of undesirable thinking patterns plus the effect of planetary alignment will be an area when we will know it is time to open up an understanding of the outer galaxies, rather than just a partial understanding directed toward our planet.

We Have the Power

In taking into consideration the power of those present upon the earth plane, it is our responsibility—the ability to respond to the situation calling for a higher form of spiritual awareness—to call upon Higher Planes of Existence, the Flame, the Light, or Source for guidance and support.

We can attune to that in our way of understanding, and recognize it as the part of the higher expression of the great and magnificent oneness of many universes in direct correlation.

We are all a part of a great society of humanity and spirit. But even greater than that, we are a part of the society of the universe of which we do and will play an even more important role.

The Suns of God came unto the sons and daughters of humanity, and mingled among them, lifting humankind into higher vibrations until a few individuals could recognize personal relationship with the Creator, and desired greater fellowship.

This pattern has been repeated over and over on the earth plane. Wave after wave of humanity went through the many periods of cyclic rebirth.

The Spiritual Youth

We are going to emphasize more and more, for individuals of spiritual integrity who have well-trained minds, who are open to soul energy, to release through their particular school of learning—the discipline and academic creative nature—something which will appeal to the "spiritual youth" of the world.

The "young people do not want to be identified with the past."

20

No matter how good the past was, most young people do not want anything of the outmoded and traditional. Their cry is, "We want a sense of newness, something we can identify ourselves with. It has to be something of the now."

What is it the youth are seeking? Youth want a sense of newness.

They certainly can identify with the Space Age and the ongoing probes into outer space. Of greater significance is the probe into the realms of inner space. The importance, the timeliness, and the sense of universal need that is supplied in the concept of the Spiritual Unity of Nations (S.U.N.) will challenge them.

Unity is going to be emphasized more and more.

Groups as Rays of the Sun

We often think of the numerous groups under different mantles and different names as sun rays. None of them are, of course, the sun itself, but rays of the Light—sun rays.

Groups are all part and parcel of the growing formation of the world servers. The idea of working toward the spiritual unity of nations can, if handled properly, be so powerful that it will override all present prohibitive elements expressed on Earth.

Eventually, the consciousness of humanity will want to know more and more about the progressive concept of the spiritual unity of the nations because spiritual power is the only power that can unite.

We look upon all the past efforts of bygone teachers, teachings, churches, societies, and groups as stepping stones toward the fulfillment of the greatest need of all—to unify by the God power, the spiritual power.

The nations will begin to come into an urgency to change. Their leaders attempt to solve their problems, but they cannot. Only spiritual power, divine love, and wisdom can unify the peoples of the world, the nations of the world. In so working in that direction, Hierarchy is behind the New Age servers.

Elder Brothers and Sisters

The Elder Brothers and Sisters of the race are all working for this goal.

They have had to wait until the coming of the Aquarian Age before they can release these powerful dynamic energies to bring about the divine alchemy, and dispense those qualities—those new interpretations that will appeal to people everywhere, even the people who have no particular religious or spiritual inclinations.

This universal message has just appeal to the religionist, politician, scholar, scientist, to the astronaut and cosmonaut and the leaders of all different ideologies.

The one unifying power. Is this a Utopian dream, we ask? How can we fit into such a cosmic plan?

Many individuals will have an opportunity to be called, called out of the crowd to listen to the cosmic voice, the voice that rings with the truths of infinitude, a universal message, a global message, a message that carries within its wings true enlightenment of man as a soul and his garments of light.

The purpose of life is to be able to unwind the mysteries of the past, the present and the future, to blaze the trail for the humanities that are to come. We must have a vision that will enable us in 10,000 years or more to look back and say, "We did our part, we kept the faith, we won because we stood shoulder to shoulder with the Hierarchy, the Light."

We belong to a new humanity, born again beyond personality, beyond nationalism.

Our message is to sound a clarion call and deliver a mighty challenge to the world, born again to a universal awareness. We are not concerned with the establishment or re-establishment of a new and updated religion. We should not be concerned with creating any more organizations. Visionary messengers of the Great Light are needed to blaze forth a vision that will find its way eventually into global awareness, with a consciousness of constructive, positive, dynamic living.

The waters of Truth from Aquarius are pouring out on all humankind.

Change is Required

When any person desecrates and pollutes their physical body and environment, they are violating the laws of the family of God and their own divine nature.

This is a truth enlightened humankind is coming to understand. When they put chemical compounds together that bring an imbalance to the natural flow of nature, the atmosphere within and without becomes inharmonious with natural law.

Natural law—the only true absolute law there is— demands changing form. When individuals recognize this there shall again be harmony in the dimensions of land, water, and sky. This comes through individual and group harmony, working together to bring all actions upon the Earth into harmony with law and order.

All of the points thus far described are but mere points of light that come together to form an overall image of the vision Deity has for humanity.

In essence, the vision Deity has for us is one of unity, of peace and love between peoples and nations, of sharing of resources, of working together for the betterment of all humankind.

The more of us that take this vision to heart, and do our part to manifest it into reality, the sooner each one of us will have unlimited peace, joy, and personal fulfillment.

The Plan

We as world servers are destined to assist Hierarchy in building a new Earth civilization on a higher octave.

An increasing number of groups are beginning to respond to this universal perspective, acknowledging their own soul or spiritual cell as an outpost of Deity itself—a cosmic spore.

Deity is seeking to express itself through each individual. No wonder the Great World Teacher said, "The Kingdom of Heaven is within you." We carry either our heaven or our hell in our own consciousness. But if we choose light, if we choose heaven, if we choose a freedom, then that entitles us to this enlightened insight into the mystery of being.

The Absolute Law operates on all levels of spirit, and has the same ultimate goal: to bring harmony throughout the universe and the individual being, moving into perfect relationship with his source.

There must be an accounting somewhere in people's nature as they abide by law. Obedience to the law brings peace and harmony in the individual manifestations of creativity.

Their innate longing is to be in harmony with their higher self and God's nature.

Idealism of Youth

The rebellion of our young generation symbolizes the hunger and thirst of the entire human race as it makes its transition from the older order into the new.

Youth is idealistic, reaching for dynamic change in diversified ways they see as progressive. They are impatient with the slow evolution of law that has been the norm for hundreds of years, for each generation has its ideals nurtured in the young populace.

The youth of the world will mature to understand that positive, constructive energy brings progressive change. There are those among the young, potentially great leaders who want to change, to move into more humane and spiritually rewarding paths.

Criticizing the old order without intelligent analysis and recommended positive change to improve the status quo ends up bringing only more frustration. Vacuums have a way of being filled with like forces circling around it. Nothing stays static for long.

Change on any level must have a rational and positive purpose, and the Aquarian Age will manifest into a great international cooperation through the efforts of our young New Age visionaries.

Can we conceive that the carrying out of God's orders would be done without thought of the minutest details, the most important assignment in two thousand years for the earth plane?

The pattern of responsibility is given to levels of Hierarchy. Humanity has been indoctrinated by their communication with the forces of God's various levels of authority. God plants ideas into the imagination, the mind, and functioning individual consciousness. Authority is delegated on many levels, in heaven and on Earth.

The Plan Has Three Major Thrusts

1. Political: to develop and establish an international consciousness by making people aware that they collectively form part of one humanity, irrespective of nation, race, color, language, or stage occupied on the evolutionary path. A spirit of international interdependence and cooperation should be promoted. In this respect, the tendency towards nations, racial superiority, antagonism, and international competition for world resources still constitute active barriers. This should make way for a brotherhood of nations based on mutual need, support, understanding, tolerance, helpfulness, goodwill, and sharing of the resources so generously provided by nature.

There already exists a movement in this direction that is being demonstrated in several respects, of which the establishment of the United Nations is the most obvious. Although this elementary organization has so far proved to be in many instances serving as a forum for the propagation of rivalry rather than of goodwill and improved human relations, it is nevertheless an indication of an underlying spirit aimed at synthesis.

2. Religious: to establish a better worldwide understanding of the nature of the subjective realms; of the duality of human existence; of the spiritual life, and the immortality of the soul; of the presence on higher levels of the Great Ones, arranged in their many hierarchical orders. The ultimate objective is a fellowship of religions, and the gradual appearance of a world faith, which in its broader concepts will be able to encompass all humanity.

3. Scientific: to coordinate those working on the many aspects of the exact sciences, and simultaneously working on a close collaboration with the rapidly expanding science of psychology. These should be further united by a joint educational program to awaken awareness of the new concepts now unfolding.

At long last, science is becoming aware of the existence of the etheric world. There are still conservatives trying to hold back, but they will find it impossible to resist the flood of evidence which is opening up new research and discovery in both etheric and other spheres of science. This may temporarily lead to a period of imbalance, with researchers vying with each other to publish ever more fantastic claims, which will not always be substantiated by factual experiment and observation. This will only be a passing phase. What matters is that science is now entering the New Era, and that both the subjective and exact sciences will become more intimately related.

Healing the Planet

This represents the essence of our world group meditation work service. Daily concentration of individuals is needed to sustain the positive energy projected into the mental ethers. The power of the world is infinite if the motive is for the ultimate benefit of all.

We ask you to assist in cooperation with other like-minded individuals, projecting love and light energy to all parts of the world on a daily basis. Our collective mental visualization can be alive, strong, and powerful—its aggregate action can serve invaluable assistance in creating positivity on all levels of the world society. Well-intentioned individuals meditating every day can create a universal chain of positive visualization and affirmation. Our daily meditative procedure symbolizes an active extension of the universal master-mind principle: "If two or more among you gather in harmony and share a common benevolent purpose, it shall be done."

Through the power of creative visualization, we can come together in peace, for healing of the races, for the healing of the nations, for the uniting of diverse paths sharing in unison and seeking a united endeavor toward light and love that blends all things into spiritual oneness. It is truly the time for all of us to work harmoniously in close cooperation in the worldwide assimilation of light and love into the mass consciousness.

How can we meditate for the benefit of the planet? Create an image of a large pyramid of light over the Earth. Inside the pyramid, envision world leaders—of all nations, religions, and philosophies—economic, financial and political officials—sitting in a large circle holding hands (symbolizing unity and goodwill for all peoples).

Please encourage your friends, relatives, and members of your religious and philosophical groups to meditate with us and link together our symbolic pyramids and further strengthen the bonds of friendship and worldwide goodwill.

BLESS ALL! "Darkness is simply the absence of light. So that which is of darkness disappears when sufficient light is generated and sent forth. Remember the first fiat of creation: "Let there be light." Now is the time for that proclamation from every willing participant in the world. Stand firm in the realization of the bright light that comes to you. Be in the vanguard of projecting new light. Love enfolds you and the plan is being fulfilled. Rest assured that uplifting of human consciousness comes as surely as the dawn!

The law governing world thought projection is simple —everyone wins. We are for the sustaining of all kingdoms —from the mineral to the cosmic. The multiplicity of realms exists so individual entities can evolve to the light, not by the light.

The Plan Has Been Initiated

It is inevitable that the S.U.N. ideals shall manifest— but when? Simply, when enough unity-minded people who care enough to actively participate in implementing their beliefs into action.

The plan is new, yet holding the same theme of common heritage of all world religions that Jesus, Muhammad, the Buddha, and all great spiritual teachers of the ages brought forth.

The Hierarchy has never given up in thrusting these concepts into the minds of receptive listeners. Individuals in all walks of life have heard the voice of unity from many representatives and wished they could do something concrete about its creation. It only needs one individual who knows the extent of his or her power and influence to spread the vision of the unity of all nations, the original concept based on the teachings of the ageless wisdom.

Esoteric philosophy, the science of the soul, halts the soul and therefore exalts the vision of unity. One person with courage and God are a majority. You may be that person becoming the Light of the World.

When a few other people also catch the vision of unity, it shall spread like the wings of an eagle spreading over the Earth. The simple invocation that was given in the 50's shall again be in the voices of earnest people. It shall be whispered in quiet moments of communion. "Oh Light of God, illumine our minds. O Love of God, fill our hearts. Oh Power of God, direct our will. Let light, love, and power enlighten mankind." When a thousand people utter that prayer daily, with sincerity and emotion, the momentum of light shall be virtually unstoppable.

Men and women will commit themselves to unity in diversity and then go onto the highways and byways of the world and spread the Word. And the Word shall have power and take precedence over all smaller visions and the goal of world peace shall become a reality.

By our perpetually planting the spiritual seed of World Unity and Sister/Brotherhood, and by each of us living every day of the year nurturing that seed growing within us, the universal awareness throughout the world will grow brighter, and the often used term of "The Light" will take on a greater and more universal significance

Let us attempt to live every day of the years ahead with a universal, altruistic feeling and attitude.

The result of these tendencies is a general movement toward better human relations and consequently greater synthesis. All this is leading to a wonderful new revelation, which will bring about radical and beneficial changes in human existence. New light will be given to humankind altering our outlook and living conditions, and inaugurating the New Age.

Peace Among Nations

This group and international unity is the ultimate goal of humankind. This is the development within the family of humanity that should be concentrated upon.

There is an inner oneness to our outer differences. Through individualization, men and women have developed multi-faceted skills that improve life upon Earth. It was not for the personal aggrandizement of individuals, but originally meant to enrich the lives of the group, to bring the various talents to the common sharing of group conscious-ness, to enhance and enrich life together. Individual personality lends variety and purpose to the balance of the meeting and sharing of bringing forth the law of love.

To what purpose does humanity develop their talents if it cannot be shared with those who hear and respond to those talents?

Individuals hear within their souls the sounds of the universe, they see with their spiritual eye the beauty existing for them, and they commune with their Creator on that level. As they share their discovery of inner beauty, they correspondingly are enriched. Humankind everywhere needs this fellowship to balance the universal energy as it creates fields of energy around them.

This is fulfillment of the law of love in group activity, destined to manifest on the physical plane, ultimately bringing Heaven to Earth.

We must again seek a union of interest and ideals, to unify on the foundation of diversity.

If the people of the world will contribute their energy and time to the new thrust of the Spiritual Unity of Nations, international peace can be achieved in our lifetime.

If visionaries and workers promote unification through education at all levels, particularly through communication systems, the positive impact upon the world would be unbelievable.

The common people of the world would be assisted the most, since world peace is a shared common motivation for all peoples. They want an environment in which they can live and prosper in peace, productivity that gives them dignity, and pride in accomplishment, harmony, and acceptance, as well as freedom from fear.

Peace Among Individuals

These are the tenets that small groups throughout the world are promoting in homes, in spiritual light groups, in business, in public places, wherever two or three are gathered together. The theme has a common thread: to learn to work together and project light and love to all of humanity.

God does not put labels upon creation, so why should any person label his or her neighbor?

A true universalist is a person who recognizes that God loves and serves humanity, regardless of lineage, culture, or belief.

Christ consciousness is energy. God Consciousness is energy. An energy that signifies the truth within one's being that demonstrates love is truth, and love and truth are active manifestations of God.

Individuals know that they know. Utilizing the power of the Word can only put into human language a definition of a knowledge and wisdom that exists, a power that is and has created humans with the potential of greatness.

Gender Equality

In Genesis 1:3, it is stated, "And God said, 'Let there be light,' and there was light." Let us see what light we can throw on the awakening of our potentials in order to balance our intellect and intuition.

The "light" referred to here does not mean light from the sun—objective light—but spiritual light—light of reality. All realities are spiritual. Only by using the power of thinking does the mind become enlightened. Only by thought does the soul develop. Only by ideas does the mind receive inspiration. Only by inspiration can the light within the soul illuminate the highways and byways of our lives. When spiritual light dawns upon the individual, its nature and quality is clearly understood by the mind because of our indwelling Higher Self—the Spirit.

In Cosmic Consciousness, Will, which is masculine, and Understanding, which is feminine, is always in creative equilibrium. Therefore, when our will affirms according to the wisdom of the understanding—when intellect and intuition work together—we can make no mistakes in our thought creations. This is the underlying secret of success.

It must be borne in mind, however, that before making any decisions, it is wise to stand back, look at our thoughts, and ask ourselves if we have wisely discriminated between our thoughts—placing the good thoughts in our world of active living and thinking, and placing the bad or incongruous thoughts in the realm of the unusable, and so to be forgotten. It is by following this practice that an orderly mentality fills the whole mind full of light.

Equal Partnerships Existed Before

Riane Eisler, in her groundbreaking *The Chalice and the Blade*, states that both the Bible and the Tao Te Ching make references to a time when man and woman coexisted in a harmonious partnership, where the feminine was revered. This observation leads her to her "Cultural Transformation Theory" in which Eisler theorizes that humanity originally was partnership oriented and peaceful in its social organization, and that after a chaotic period initiated by the invasion of a warrior people, the dominator society was imposed on them and has continued to serve as the model for nations to the present.

Riane Eisler contends that for there ever to be a real peace on Earth, we must return to a partnership model of society where both sexes are truly equal, and points to various other sources which share her view. The futurists Robert Jungk, David Loye, and John Platt, as well as the Baha'i Universal House of Justice, all see the connection between true equality for men and women and world peace.

Going a step further, Eisler states that although it may seem a daunting task, all great causes had their modest beginnings in the mind(s) of only a few, but a relentless pursuit for social justice eventually brought them into fruition. She cites as examples the abolition of slavery, the movement from monarchial governments toward democracies, as well as many other social reforms gained over the past several hundred years.

Additionally, it seems that the ultimate symbol of the feminine, Earth itself, is rising in rebellion as well. The years of unchecked degradation of the planet is resulting in serious consequences which have become more widely recognized as people are literally finding evidence of them in their own backyards. Ecological imbalance is the cause for the dramatic change in our weather patterns and climate.

This can all be attributed to a lack of respect of the feminine. The unenlightened attitudes of governments which enact laws that deny women access to family planning and education and encourage procreation are a major contributing factor in overpopulation. Even if family planning were more universally accessible, Eisler reports, population experts are warning that for a curbing of population growth to succeed, roles for women besides that of housekeeping and parenting must be honored by the society in which they live, and must be available and promoted alongside birth control education and guarantees of reproductive freedom.

The Return of the Feminine

One of the main causes for disharmony upon the earth plane is that nations and religions have forgotten that basic law of male and female balance. Male dominance has prevailed and still prevails in almost the entire world.

For the past 5,000 years, civilization has been dominated by the masculine, both secularly and spiritually. This male dominance has resulted from the conqueror mentality that has dominated this period.

But in the recesses of humanity's collective unconscious, there lives a memory of a more gentle and peaceful
time when men and women lived in partnership with each
other.

Archaeological discoveries are revealing that there
existed thousands of years of peaceful prosperity where
civilization was not dominated by the male. These
discoveries are supported by the images and writings that
have survived from the earliest periods of recorded history.
The ancient Greeks (i.e., Plato, who wrote of the civilization
of Atlantis) told of such societies in their prose and poetry,
and evidence is mounting that these stories are not merely
fictional accounts as has long been believed. An example of
such stories that were originally thought to be pure myth is
the story of Troy. Not until an archaeologist by the name of
Heinrich Schliemann discovered the city of Troy under
centuries of earth was it accepted that the ancient Greek tale
of this great city was a true accounting of an historic place.

The male ego must give way to the pyramid energy of
Divine Earth Mother, and men must recognize within
themselves the feminine aspect of their own natures. In
time, humankind shall become androgynous beings, with
male and female aspects perfectly balanced in their physical
as well as etheric bodies, as Jesus exemplified.

The Piscean Age represented the feminine aspect of
universal energy, the Aquarian Age the masculine.
However, the effect of this is that during the Piscean Age,
men became defensive and generally overcompensated by
taking more power than they rightfully deserved, as they
responded to their emotions more than their intellect.

The Aquarian Age—which activates the intellect more
than the emotions—will see many more women taking
much more active roles in local, national, and international

affairs. The feminine energy will be greatly felt in political and cultural leadership roles.

The quality of cooperation of masculine and feminine energies will be greatly increasing as the Aquarian Age progresses. The universe is constantly striving for balance. In order to balance the scales, women must now assume responsibility in fulfilling their rightful role in the evolution of humanity upon Earth.

Women in leadership positions will flourish in this dynamic, progressive period of history.

Woman brings man to balance, and brings the world to justice and truth.

Ancient Wisdom of the Sister-Brotherhood

From the Ancient Wisdom of the Brotherhood, coming out of Egypt, there are certain teachings in regard to the Feminine aspect.

"The Mother takes her role in the entire physical universe. Through the Mother, continuity of the Flame—of life, culture, and the blissful awareness of the Father—is preserved from one generation to the next."

The ancient Wisdom has spoken to present-day crisis. Women must come forth to fulfill their destiny.

For the plan of the Hierarchy to be realized, it is imperative that the idea of male superiority be extinguished and the feminine be returned to her rightful place alongside the masculine as the co-creative principle.

The year 2000 marked the beginning of the feminine millennium. The belief in a male God has been replaced with a "kinder, gentler" image of a supreme divine intelligence which nurtures all Creation.

The present dominant concept of a male Creator harkens back to prehistory when early humans sought to explain the source of various phenomena of which they had no understanding. Their perception gave mysterious meaning to things, which we take for granted today; the motion of the moon around the Earth, the changing patterns of the constellations in the night sky, and the changing of the seasons, to name a few.

To this early human mind, a god with human attributes was reassuring and logical, and the nature of human relationships became the model for explaining humanity's relationship with the Divine. Hence, the idea of God as a father figure arose. The father principle continued to be a major aspect in various religious philosophies and eventually came into use by initiates of the Mysteries as a tool to invoke higher plane assistance in response to a crisis.

Christ Urged a Restoration

Two thousand years ago, the incarnation of a spiritual Master initiated an effort to return humanity to the partnership ideal and restore peace on Earth. Jesus' mission was to bring the vibration of love and compassion to a humanity who had for too long lived with fear and oppression.

Love and compassion are considered "feminine" emotions. Indeed, emotions in general are considered by many to be the realm of the feminine. The spiritual Hierarchy saw the need for these principles to be re-indoctrinated into the consciousness of the human species and sent Jesus as an emissary to teach them.

The purpose of Christ's teachings was to restore balance between the feminine and masculine. Jesus focused on the Feminine Mysteries which reveal the subconscious and subjective aspects of life. These teachings are revealed in the use of images and language which are symbolically feminine (i.e., the moon, caves, rivers, female animals such as mares and sows, and various birds) and emphasizing such feminine attributes as compassion and the practice of service. All this points to the feminine as a "profoundly significant" force in the universe that needs to be restored to its rightful place alongside, and in equal partnership with, the masculine.

Andrews states that "the scriptures are an allegory for the redemption of the Divine Feminine" and their purpose was to lay the foundation to accomplish this task. It is now up to us to take the necessary steps to accomplish it. It may not come without a struggle, but we are equipped with the tools to succeed, as we, in fact, have begun to demonstrate.

There is Hope

There is hope. Humanity is evolving—in positive ways —in spite of attempts by some to maintain the status quo.

We can choose our next step. Add to that the fact that our social consciousness is becoming more partnership oriented, and that science is "focusing more on relationships than on hierarchies," and we have the recipe for a new model of male-female relationships.

Humanity is beginning to comprehend the need for balance between the feminine and the masculine, and is choosing in ever-increasing numbers partnership in relationships, both individual and global.

Eisler indicates that there is a growing awareness of the ideal of partnership, and that science is discovering the possibilities for the expansion of consciousness of our species and the subsequent evolution of society.

Scholars and theorists are predicting a rebalancing of the roles of men and women where there is equal sharing of the responsibilities of child-rearing as well as career opportunities. This will result in a healthier society and economy and humanity will begin to realize its full potential. This in turn will lead to the end of the threat of war and the degradation of the planet, not to mention the more personal social problems we are faced with today.

Section 3:
Ancient Secrets
Revealed

We Have Always Had Lights of the World

Many names have been given to Central Intelligence, including the Godhead, the Central Sun, and Universal Mind. From this center of power comes direction of all that is.

There is nothing that is not operated by law. Once this vibration is incorporated into the consciousness of the next level of energy in the universe, this level of authority puts God's desires into operation.

God has never left his manifestation—humanity—upon the Earth without spiritual leaders.

Humanity has listened to the great beings who dedicated their lives to bringing forth the world as directed by the Hierarchy under the command of God.

From the dawn of antiquity when the Enlightened Ones brought wisdom and truth to the planet Earth, giving humanity hope, there has always been a remnant of Masters upon the earth plane.

Slowly but surely, each time the great world light is brought to light on the Earth, the Earth has made that much more progress into the realm of light, increasing its vibration, for the Earth is truly a living entity of God just as the living body of humankind.

We All Have the Potential

Throughout evolution there has been the purified lineage of wisdom running through a certain group of humanity, sustaining the essence of their heritage. The Great Masters of truth, from the Godhead to the present day, have reserved the seed that—when the designated time was upon the Earth—germinated into mastership.

We all have the potential of becoming through training in self-mastery.

In previous incarnations, the Masters have met and overcome, and through their accomplishment of overcoming have developed paranormal comprehension of universal law.

During the periods of rest between rebirths, these Masters' souls, with developed power to look upon the future, return to that field of endeavor assisting humankind to evolve into even higher development.

Endowed with rare gifts of knowledge, spiritualized to the point of perfect control over the mental, emotional, physical, and material, these great souls of the Egyptian Masters from the ancient heritage of Atlantis founded the Coptic mystery schools in the land of Egypt, so abundant with humanity's spiritual history. For 1900 years, they have safeguarded the great truths entrusted to them by the lineage of the White Brotherhood to the Essene Order.

Those enlightened souls who have called upon God, and purified thoughts and deeds, can penetrate the veil and understand the plan as unfolded by Hierarchy. More and more individuals worldwide have reached this point of development.

When the majority of humanity understands the purpose and plan of the Godhead, as carried forth by the Hierarchical Board, many souls will become the Light of the World. This is the reason for enlightenment. This is the cause of the giving of information through the written word.

This is coming by command of the Hierarchy through enlightened individuals everywhere whose spirits have yielded to the will of the Father-Mother God. Their understanding, purity of heart, and trust in God's guidance through many lifetimes has brought them this responsibility for this message. It is a combined effort of many enlightened souls who have learned through trial and error that God is love and cares for His own.

Jesus Christ

When the Christ Consciousness came upon the man Jesus as He was baptized by His beloved cousin, John, whom he knew and loved dearly, it was God's way of showing humanity they had the power to come into their own heritage as perfected Christed beings.

Jesus was taken to Egypt as a child because there were enlightened teachers in Egypt who could reveal to Him "The Word."

In the days of the preparation for the descending of the Christ Consciousness upon the pure body of the man Jesus, there was much controversy—much disturbance in the country of Jesus' birth.

Individuals were limited in their understanding of the spiritual energy around them, as the plan unfolded upon the earth plane so designed by the Hierarchy. With limited knowledge and understanding, many myths about the reason for the incarnation of the Christ power were created.

The Kingdom, as envisioned by the Godhead, must be only a spiritual one, coming into the hearts of people as love vibration.

Christ as a Pattern for Humanity

The Christ as manifested for three years through the man Jesus brought the spiritual law to mankind. It was a pattern in which humanity could bring love and light to the world.

Grasping for security in the pressure of darkness in humanity's minds, in that period of history, those who saw the vision of the spiritual law as exemplified by Jesus built an aura around the bringer of the law and put Him on a pedestal.

This created a fabric of worship around the messenger rather than the message.

Never at any time did Jesus ask to be venerated. "Only my Father in Heaven is perfect," He declared to his followers. He was to be the way-shower—the exemplification of that pattern of purity and goodness by which mankind could build their own lives. "You shall do greater works that I do," He declared. "I am son of man," He kept repeating over and over again.

Accepting their own Christ consciousness as demonstrated by Jesus, it must be impressed upon the true visionaries that individuals are totally responsible for their personal actions. Deeds of prior selfishness must be worked through and balanced by the law of karma. Each person is responsible for his or her own personal thoughts, words, and deeds.

The Piscean message came to save people from themselves, not through depending on the personage of Christed Jesus. One could only redeem oneself as one forgave oneself and others, and expressed the law of unconditional love to the greatest of one's ability.

The appearing of the Light of the World will not come until humanity opens their hearts to the true universal message that the Master Jesus brought forth. Christians everywhere must emphasize their similarities, not their differences. Christians should be those who recognize the workings of God in the minds and hearts of all religious followers everywhere. There should be no distinction. Christ through Jesus said, "I lift all men unto me." This was intended to include all of humanity.

Jesus was trained by spiritually advanced teachers who understood the power of the Godhead as manifested throughout the universe.

An accurate record was kept of that training of Jesus' development in preparation for receiving Christhood. At the allotted time, those ancient records will be revealed to God's people. They will be removed from their hiding place, as well as records that came from ancient Atlantis into the hearts of souls eons ago.

This time schedule is in the hands of men and women throughout the earth plane. When enough world light is anchored upon the planet Earth, the revelation of such laws shall come forth.

At this time, humanity shall be called to make an accounting of their Sunship. Individuals shall demonstrate their responsibility as a Light of the World, accepting their inheritance and acknowledging truth.

Symbology of Jesus

In ancient symbology, each of the twelve disciples of Jesus are synonymous with one of the twelve houses of the Zodiac, representing the twelve powers of mind that are to be reached by the different levels of consciousness of humanity. The disciples were chosen to include the consciousness spectrum of the human race, for in the higher planes they represent all creation. As above, so below.

Jesus the Christ was devoted to bringing the spiritual message entrusted to him by God and thereby redeem humankind from their spiritual shortcomings. Jesus and His disciples left humankind a heritage more valuable than any earthly treasures—the gift of teachings carrying words of power and truth. Accent has been on the cross and the crucifixion rather than His ascension to Christed inner consciousness. He taught that there was an inherent inner awareness that should be developed and applied. By hiding from humanity the one condition of his salvation—personal responsibility for the assimilation and application of thoughts and actions—valuable sections of Jesus's teachings have been kept hidden, along with many records of His activities. It is now time for many of these records to be revealed.

The Brahmans, Buddhists, and Muhammadans understood Jesus's divinity and kept in-depth records. Records exist in Istanbul (Constantinople), Rome, and Egypt, but only in the Library of Alexandria was the complete history of Jesus kept. The Essenes knew of the possible burning of the Alexandrian Library, and were able to secure duplicate records to be placed in hiding before the destruction. The true revelation of Jesus's ministry on Earth must be known to prevent humankind from making the same mistakes again and delaying the personal purification of the individual in preparation for his or her now Christhood and soul liberation. The hidden records, when found in Egypt, will reveal that Jesus did not die on the cross, nor did He suffer on the cross. By protecting himself in a higher state of consciousness—suspended animation— He was above pain in the physical body, and therefore did not suffer. Jesus learned these self-mastery skills in Egypt as a young man.

The demonstration of His entire ministry did not violate any natural law. He utilized spiritual laws to live and serve as a prototype for humanity to imitate. Hamid Bey—by his demonstration of his abilities of 5,000 + burials alive— dramatically illustrated that Jesus would also possess this same technique. A High Priest has left a written account of what transpired on the day of Jesus's crucifixion—the information can be read in Rome and Constantinople.

The Jewish Sabbath dawned and moved toward noon. All three of the men who hung on crosses on Golgotha Hill were still alive. One of the rules of keeping the Sabbath holy was that no criminal should remain upon his cross past the hour of 11. Each criminal was to be taken down and his legs broken, hastening death.

At the crucifixion scene, arguing ensued among Jesus's enemies. Jesus had said He would rebuild his physical body in three days. With His strange powers, they thought he might do so. Stabbing him with a spear would take care of Him, the soldiers argued, and they did so. Blood and water poured from Jesus's body wound, proving He was not dead. Blood sinks into a central pool at death, and ceases to flow. Crucifixion witnesses failed to comprehend this reality. A group of Essenes came forward and claimed the body from the cross. The small Essene group wrapped His body in white, and were ordered to take it to the tomb. The door was sealed and guards stationed outside.

Jesus's advanced consciousness reawakened in a physical body that had not died, exercising again the Essene art of suspended animation, as other Masters in the past had done. Jesus performed this feat in the tomb, rebuilding and healing the flesh of His physical body. Certain Essenes were located near the tomb, and at the proper time, rolled away the stone and removed the Messiah. The guards aroused from sleep found an empty tomb. The guards, justifying their reasons for falling asleep on the job, were personally responsible for the ascension story.

After He was removed from the tomb, Jesus appeared to His disciples, revealing His miraculous healing.

The Rest of the Story

We know that at the time of His crucifixion, Christ ascended into a state of heavenly consciousness, and remained for three days in communion with the Cosmic Spirit. During this time, He received new light regarding the problems of humanity, and saw that His work upon the Earth must be continued for a number of years.

During the crucifixion, Jesus had the realization that it would be expedient to go into a secret retreat in Egypt, and there concentrate upon explaining His philosophy to a few chosen Masters, who would preserve its purity and take charge of its further dissemination among humanity.

We know that Christ's mission was to convince the world that the idea of limitation is but a faulty human concept, and that limitation has no cosmic reality.

The term 'God' stands for all beings, and God is love. The illusion of evil is due simply to a limited scope of perspective. This and many other theories will become clear when we learn to place the correct interpretation upon the parables of Jesus.

The fact that we ourselves are cosmic beings advancing toward universal consciousness will become increasingly evident as we ponder the teachings of the Great Master. The so-called miracles performed by Christ were, in reality, deeds done in accordance with a higher and more complete knowledge of cosmic law.

When He said, "The things that I do, ye can do also," He meant that all of us will eventually attain a Universal Consciousness, and gain the ability to perform feats that we formerly may have regarded as miracles. Each of us, He taught, will come to the point where we can say with deep and certain knowledge, "I AM THAT I AM." To Him, His crucifixion was a symbol of humankind's ignorance, and He felt only tolerance and compassion toward those who had laid their hands upon Him. "Forgive them," He said, "for they know not what they do."

Jesus permitted the apparent physical sacrifice at the crucifixion because He realized that the general state of consciousness prevailing at that time could best be reached in this dramatic way. Since the highest value was laid upon human life, He knew that people would never forget a sacrifice of this kind. They would continue to think about the man who had laid down His life for humanity, and gradually they would come to understand and appreciate His philosophy of divine love in expression.

Jesus wanted His teachings accepted. After His survey of world conditions, He realized that the enactment of this great resurrection would be the most effective means of arousing international interest in His teachings. It is true that He had touched some hearts during the period of His ministry, but His following was very small, just a few devoted disciples whom He felt would be benefited by an outstanding example of renunciation.

He challenged the world by His survival on the cross. Now, after over 2,000 years, this challenge still stands, and Christ and His philosophy are spoken of in every country. Gradually, inevitably, the true significance of His life is becoming comprehensible. His crucifixion is justified.

Thinking that the drama of Jesus's crucifixion ended most fittingly with His ascension, the scribes determined to preserve the powerful effect of His crucifixion by saying nothing of what actually took place after the Master's body was removed from the cross.

The storms and earthquakes described as occurring at that crucifixion time are symbolic of the overwrought emotions of the people. They were in a mental and emotional state of disturbance, confusion, and fear. Without understanding it, they sensed the importance of the event and were filled with a deep sense of anxiety.

The Messiah of the Old Testament

The Messiah of the Old Testament, Moses (the original name is Mosche), was of Egyptian birth, a reality not well known. He was, in fact, the son of the Pharaoh of that day —a ruler during the 8th dynasty. Mosche's ideal was that of sacred justice, unlike his father, who treated the Israelites so horribly that the Prince Mosche attempted to be their protector.

The Israelites accepted, worshipped, and obeyed Moses, this man of God. Having been enslaved for so many years, they had not acquired the discipline required of a progressive new nation. Moses laid down for them the laws for the foundation of this great nation. It took many years to establish the pattern of the universal consciousness within Moses' own being. This Avatar let go of his bodily form when the mission of his lawgiving was fulfilled. The physical remains of Moses and Jesus presently lie in a hidden chamber in the Pyramid of Giza.

Jesus the Christ, being the manifestation of the attributes of wisdom and love, was the Way-shower for all humanity living in the visible or objective world. These two attributes, considered as one, could be called the Universal Principle, and is truly universal. It is this principle which beautifies and spiritualizes the soul of humanity, for the attribute of love is within the comprehension of every human being.

Humanity lives in the visible world to learn to be above hatred, to be above jealousies, to be forgiving, to live in the awareness of the Presence of God, and to realize that "as ye give, so shall ye receive."

Jesus Lived On

Jesus lived on for an additional 214 years after the crucifixion. He continued to visit His disciples and other followers for the last 200 years of His life to continuously encourage them in faith and power.

When Jesus passed from this sphere of life at age 247, the Essenes, who had the necessary knowledge required, petrified His body.

This ceremony is quite elaborate and detailed. It was carried out at the Sphinx and the large Pyramid of Giza at Jesus's age of 247, the same location where He took His initiation as a young man of 12 when He was initiated as Saint Issa.

During Issa's (Jesus's) life in Egypt—from age 33 onward—He spent extensive periods of time near the Sphinx and Giza complex. At the end of each day, He rejoiced with great pleasure in His communion with Spirit. He was growing steadfastly in His inner knowing of the God awareness. He utilized the pyramid energy as a power chamber to augment His already powerful personal force field. He needed this additional supplement of energy, for He daily took its energy into Himself as He contemplated the pyramid's beneficence. He often went to the Sakkara Temples near Cairo, and taught the Egyptian priests how to heal, fusing his mind-power extension to cure their physical body ailments.

Mary Magdalene was also with Jesus in Egypt during intermittent time periods, being His most dedicated disciple. They often spent many hours together meditating and sharing. They married and had children. Mary Magdalene eventually established a church in France, at Rennes-le-Château.

At the time of Jesus's life in Egypt after the crucifixion, the capstone was in place on the pyramid apex, gleaming white on the etheric realm.

The Importance of the Sphinx

The Sphinx and pyramid structures at Giza have significant meaning in the lives of spiritually oriented Egyptians. The Sphinx represents the material plane while the pyramid represents the spiritual plane. These great structures are connected by a secret passage that has been sealed these many centuries. The secret passage will be opened when the time is right for it to be unsealed, revealing many secrets only a few have been privileged to know. The passage seal under the Sphinx and pyramid cannot be found until humanity has started to overcome their lower nature.

The Sphinx was built after the Great Pyramid. It is the spiritual entrance to the older monuments. It is also a symbol of the individual's evolutionary progress. The Sphinx has the lower body of a lion, the upper body of a human being, the face of a man, and the head of a woman. Back of the head are two wings. This signifies that man formerly belonged to the animal kingdom, as indicated by the lion's body and the future of a god as symbolized by the wings behind the head.

Through evolution, which is motivated by suffering and the subsequent awakening of a desire for advanced wisdom, a more perfect physical body develops. Since the soul may incarnate either as a man or woman, male and female characteristics are shown on the Sphinx face and head. Each soul must exist both as a man and woman in order to achieve full development, for we must all acquire the dual qualities of intellect (symbolized by the male) and the expression of love (symbolized by the female).

The law of duality (Nature of God) is also symbolized in the Sphinx by the man's face and the woman's head. When a human being has attracted to himself a member of the opposite sex, and assimilated the necessary completing knowledge and wisdom, he is liberated from the lower self, and enjoys a new sense of spiritual freedom. In the Sphinx, this emancipation is illustrated by the presence of eagle wings at the back of the head. The wings indicate that the sixth sense has been awakened, and that man has entered into the spiritual realm. The sixth sense is the pineal gland in the back part of the head.

The Passing of a Master

In ancient times, the passing of a Master from the earth plane to higher realms was not an ordinary happening. The ritual of initiation for their transition is begun in front of the Sphinx and completed within the Great Pyramid. This initiation is designed for the ushering of a Master's soul from the physical body into the celestial realm of God Consciousness. Only the body of a Master is brought before the Sphinx, previously earthbound and now ready to find communion with the Cosmic Spirit through the ascension initiation.

The following is an explanation of the ascension ceremony of Jesus (Issa) at the age of 247 in the Great Pyramid at the Giza complex.

Three days and three nights are required for the astral body to take leave of the physical body. This is the length of time that the ascension ceremony lasts. The casket is made ready at the entrance of the Great Pyramid to receive the body of the great being. When the body has been placed within the casket, it is then borne to the King's Chamber if the Master is a man, to the Queen's Chamber if the Master is a woman.

As soon as the casket has been taken into the Grand Gallery, seven Masters are closed in the Temple, and the Master Mason seals the passage. The masters, or High Priests of the three natures of man are the ones who actually carry the body into the King's or Queen's Chamber. The three priests then separate into different chambers. The seven Masters necessary for this great ceremony are:

1. The Building Mason, the Building Master
2. The Astronomical Master, the Master of the Proceedings
3. The Astrological Master; the Master who determines the position
4. The Golden Master, the Master of Wisdom who goes into the secret chamber above the King's Chamber, which symbolizes spirituality.
5. The Sensation Master, the Master of Conscious Reasoning Power, who stays with the body
6. The Silver Master, the Master of Memory or Records, who goes into a secret chamber symbolizing the subconscious part of man
7. The Christ Consciousness, the seventh Master, present in spirit. He is the body that is lying in the sarcophagus.

When the Great Pyramid has been closed under the direction of the Master Mason and the body has been placed as indicated, the seven Masters take up their proper positions, and remain for six days in meditation. The Golden Master enters the special chamber above the King's Chamber. This chamber has never been discovered by archaeologists.

In this particular hidden chamber is kept the golden cap, which at the time of the ceremony is placed on top of the pyramid. This cap has remained hidden. The cap symbolizes the superconsciousness, or spirituality of humanity. According to ancient records, gold represents God.

While the Master of Sensation stays with the body, the Silver Master enters into the great Hall of Records, which symbolizes the subconscious mind of man. The Master Mason and the Astronomical and Astrological Masters prepare the way for the initiate's body to be taken into this great chamber. After six days of meditation, when the soul of the Master being initiated has completely passed through the golden cap and becomes One with Universal Consciousness, the cap is removed and placed again in the superconscious chamber. As soon as this is done, the outside ceremony ceases, and the silk covering—which had enveloped the Great Pyramid since the beginning of the ritual—is taken off.

The burning torches are extinguished, and the multitudes return to their homes, for the soul of the Master has been received into a heavenly state. As the people retire into the darkness of the night, a flame burns in the heart of each person, carrying the hope that someday there may be sufficient illumination for each soul to leave the darkness of this Earth, and dwell in the real eternal light.

When the initiation has been completed, the six Masters descend with the body of the seventh into the great Archive Chamber, there to begin its preservation. No mummies have been found in the Pyramid of Giza, because the Masters understood the art of petrification. This special form of preservation is used for the bodies of those whose spirits have passed into Heaven through the golden cap.

It requires three days to petrify a body, and the six Masters remain within the Pyramid for that length of time. During this period they do not leave the monument for any reason whatsoever. Food and water are brought to them through a secret passage, the location of which only the Master Mason knows.

Only Masters who have attained the Universal Consciousness can go through with the ritual in front of the Sphinx and pass into the Great Pyramid where the celestial initiation is completed.

Jesus the Christ, at the age of 247 years, was the last Master to go through with the great initiation just described, and his soul entered into a heavenly lane through the golden cap placed on top of the Pyramid of Giza.

The Perfection of the Pyramid

The pyramid monument as a whole represents perfection, and within it are chambers representing the physical, the spiritual, the superconscious, and the sub-conscious. Harmony must exist among these parts before the ideal of perfection can be achieved. Humanity is still striving to attain this harmony and arrive at the divine balance symbolized by the Great Pyramid.

As Jesus, in His youth, was initiated into the secrets of the Great White Brotherhood, known as the Essenes, so was He initiated when His soul took flight and returned to the Source of Light. Jesus's body is still in the Great Pyramid of Giza, along with Moses, who went through the same ascending initiation upon his death in the physical body at the age of 98.

Beneath this pyramid chamber where the physical remains of the two great Messiahs lie are other hidden chambers, containing a wealth of spiritual records. The "Hall of Records" sought by so many people through the ages will be opened to reveal secrets of humanity's unfolding since the dawn of time. The Word will be revealed, and made new when the hour of the Light of the World is before us.

The remains of Elijah and John the Baptist have been announced to the world to be physically present in the Coptic St. Macarius Monastery in Egypt. It is fitting, since John's body was used by the soul of Elijah during the mission of the forerunner for Christ.

Buddha

Westerners have been inclined to disregard the Buddhist teachings, declaring that Christians have the one and only truth.

The Buddha was as much a divine manifestation to the Far East as was the Christ in Palestine six centuries later. Buddha was the spiritual leader of the East, as was Christ for the West. The worship of Buddha statues have been no more deeply entrenched in the doctrine of Easterners than have some of the symbols developed by Christians.

One function of Hierarchy is to initiate Avatars— common people who are divine messengers bringing the teachings of God directly to humankind. For Westerners to pass judgment on the quality of Eastern faith is a violation of the universal Christ principle.

Each Master brought the light according to the needs of the people at that time. In the past three millennia, two major approaches were given so that the human soul could experience a particular aspect of the Divine. The manifestation of the light, intelligence, and wisdom that was embodied in the Buddha—an the example of divine love, combined with reason, as displayed in the Christ, "The Illumined One,"—pointed the way by the appeal to use interaction, mental comprehension, and wisdom. Buddha is recognized as the "Light Bearer." He presented four Noble Truths and the Eight-fold Path:

1) Right Values	5) Right Aspiration
2) Right Speech	6) Right Conduct
3) Right Modes of Living	7) Right Effort
4) Right Thinking	8) Right Absorption

Buddhism represents a foundation established for combining Buddha love and human relations each soul is striving to achieve. Buddha demonstrated in his own life these universal concepts, helping mankind understand that God was present within this moment, but also in control of the universe. The Buddhist became conscious of the God within and also aware of a universal God. This thinking represented a great revelation. Before Buddha's incarnation, humanity had not considered God as personal. This was a revolutionary thought in personal progress toward divinity. Buddha brought great enlightenment to humanity.

In the hierarchical system, the Buddha is an intermediary between Shamballa and the Hierarchy of the Masters. He is part of a Triangle of Force, the other two parts being Spirit of Peace, and the Avatar of Synthesis. These three jointly support the Christ, aiding Him with the force of Light, Love, and Power. Cooperation on all levels is required for fulfilling Christ's task as Leader of the Hierarchy and Teacher of Humanity, as he comes forth into the energies of the Aquarian Age.

Strong bonds between the Buddha, the Christ, and humanity go back throughout the ages.

King Arthur

In the ancient mysteries of the teachings of the Great Masters, one great revelation has come down through the ages to give credence to the story of the eternal search of each soul for his or her perfect, divine image.

The Holy Grail had its beginning in the far distant mists of the human beginning upon the Earth. According to some records, the earliest story of the Grail was written in Egypt. This great story depicts the individual's long search for the personal high and holy self. Having lost this perfect state, each person longs to rediscover it.

The Holy Grail, according to legend, was the cup used by Jesus and His disciples at the Last Supper. It was at this event that Jesus gave his highest and holiest teachings to his beloved disciples. There have been many facets to the legend. One dearest to Christians and spiritual searchers has been the story of King Arthur and the Knights of the Round Table. Much speculation still exists as to where the Grail Castle was located.

All known accounts are speculation, but legends have a way of being based on truth, often disguised in symbolic language for protection from the scrutinizing eyes of the uninitiated. Truth seekers have the inner knowingness to see the esoteric meaning behind the written message.

The Stories

The stories of Sir Galahad, Sir Gawain, those knights who sought the Holy Grail, are epic stories of individuals whose ideals are universal but do not have the dedication of purpose to achieve the Grail—the symbolic prize that all

men and women must find on the soul's journey back to
perfection.

King Arthur and his court is an account of the lives of
knights and ladies in the Middle Ages. The spiritual seeker
discovers that this story is exemplary of the early Mystery
Schools, cloaked in the unfolding of the long journey of the
soul seeking for inner divinity through the struggles of
earthly existence.

History states that King Arthur lived approximately
fourteen centuries ago, about 500 A.D. He was leader of the
Britons when the Anglo-Saxons invaded their homeland.
King Arthur's many acts of valor spread across Europe in
story and song.

The singers of mystical songs declared Arthur came
from the land of the "little people" (a reference to the inner,
or etheric realm), "brought to Earth by three beautiful
queens—whose names were Faith, Hope, and Love—
always representing qualities of a universal teacher."

Merlin, the Wise One, knew of the ancient teachings
coming from Lemuria, Atlantis, Babylon, and Egypt, from
Greece and Rome. His name signified the "Wondrous
One." He possessed the wisdom of the serpent (Kundalini
energy) without its guile. He could read past and future
events. Arthur and the knights were awed by his powers.

The poet tells of the stormy night at sea, when Merlin
witnessed a ship aflame from stern to stern and shining
people on the decks. Wave upon wave rolled until the ninth
wave when a naked babe was born. Merlin caught the babe
and cried, "The King!"

This is a beautiful accounting of the birth of the inner
World Light, cloaked in mystical language full of spiritual
symbolism. The Church Fathers in the first three centuries
after Christ often referred to such mysteries. The work of

the Essenes was also an integral part of these mystical writings.

Arthur Proved Himself

As a young man, Arthur already displayed rare beauty of stature and spirit, and supernatural powers. In a vision he was taken to see the Grail, guarded by virgins. Arthur participated in a midnight holy communion and saw the spiritual power contained in the Holy Vessel. He received a pure white crystal cross as a voice spoke, "Under this sign will you conquer." He then pledged his life to the service of the Grail.

Arthur proved his right to become King by removing a shining sword embedded in a great white stone. Many knights tried to retrieve the sword but were unable to wrest it from its anchor. Arthur lifted the mighty sword easily, signifying the availability of spiritual powers when needed. The stone signifies the crystallized old order. The spirit of truth is appropriately symbolized in the sword of shining valor.

Round Table

King Arthur founded the Round Table, which legend dramatically declared was symbolically the same table present at the Last Supper.

For the Knights to be accepted for one of the seats at the Round Table meant years of hard work, dedication of soul, mind, and body. It involved eating the right food, universal thinking, and deeds of valor, altruism, and love. Loyalty had to be assured. A high spiritual power wrote the name of the knight who should sit in each chair. The chair remained vacant until the perfect knight appeared.

Spiritually, every aspirant to the holy life is tested before being permitted to enter into the activities of this special inner circle. This was portrayed by Sir Galahad, who said, "It is here that I must renounce all things in order that I may gain all." An apt description of the true test of one questing for World Light Consciousness.

As Galahad met and conquered his tests, his name flashed in golden light upon the chair. Angels declared in joyous song Galahad's right to join the valiant knights, so loyal to the King. This was the way of gaining membership into the early Mystery Schools.

The Holy Grail is the story of achieving membership into the mystery of the Hierarchical teachings. The knights who presented themselves to the King, vowed to dedicate their lives to his service, to search for the Holy Grail, but were actually dedicating themselves to the World Light within.

Arthur's End

The fair Knight Lancelot came to King Arthur in his young manhood, gifted, adventuresome, idealistic, and the King and Knights accepted him into their sacred group. Though he loved Arthur, Lancelot took every opportunity to be with Queen Guinevere.

Guinevere's power over Lancelot caused him to fail in his quest for the Holy Grail. Lancelot could not forget the spiritual joy he would have earned if he had accomplished the task to which he had committed himself. He mourned this loss throughout his life.

The story of Lancelot gives evidence that the pilgrim seeking the Holy Grail who takes the path of the heart may have more trials than the one who takes the mind path as did Merlin.

It was not Merlin's activities that destroyed King Arthur's court. It was the betrayal of knights like Lancelot who let their lower emotional nature rule their lives. They were responsible for the demise of the Holy Order of the Knights of the Round Table, the scattering of the knights that Tennyson has described in the magnificent poem, "Idylls of a King," with these words, "That glorious company, the flower of all men."

As King Arthur lay mortally wounded, he commanded his faithful knight Bedivere to throw his famous Excalibur into the lake. When Bedivere finally did, after three attempts, an arm arose, grasped and held the still perfect sword aloft. It shone like brilliant shafts of light, then disappeared.

His knights took King Arthur to the lake where a barge appeared with the three beautiful queens, Faith, Hope and Love, riding upon it. The Queens uttered cries of sorrow that rang throughout the heavens. They took Arthur aboard and prepared him for the homeward journey. The mystic ship disappeared and as angelic voices rang out, King Arthur bade his new faithful disciples farewell. "The old order passeth, making way for the new. And God fulfills Himself in many ways."

Hamid Bey

Another such personage with universal spiritual focus is the one who founded the Coptic teachings in America, Hamid Bey.

He came out of the East to bring the great teachings to Western civilization from the Egyptian Inner Temples of Learning. He had been trained well to bring to this Aquarian dispensation the wisdom of Egypt—the seat of so many magnificent civilizations and cultures. The following information is a short synopsis from the fascinating account of his life as recorded in his autobiography, *My Experiences Preceding 5,000 Burials*.

Hamid Bey's Early Years

Hamid Bey recalls that at the early age of two he was curious about the ancient temples of learning. At age five, he was asking mature questions and possessed a thirst for knowledge of spiritual subjects. He learned the history of the Christian religion—focused on the original sayings of Christ—and learned that shortly after the crucifixion, followers of Christ began to build physical temples in Egypt.

Many of those temples still stand today. It is in some of these temples that the teachings and inner work of the Master Jesus are still preserved. The true Master Teachers spent time meditating and preserving the original intent of Jesus. In Egypt, Jesus learned about Christ power from the Initiate Egyptian Masters.

In his schooling, Hamid Bey learned everyone had one Father-Mother, who is God. He was required throughout his training to treat everyone as his brother or sister, for actually only one planetary family of God existed on Earth. No fear existed in his religious training. He did not know until he came to America that different sects existed because of differences in opinions about the original teachings of Christ.

Hamid's life experiences in early 1900's Egypt prepared him for his great life of service. When Hamid Bey was five years old, he had a remarkable experience. He was playing in an Egyptian street when a strange man walked up to him and smiled down at him. Hamid felt something wonderful was happening, and he felt a very strong bond with this man he had never seen before. They talked together for a few minutes, and then the man left, promising that he would return soon. This man was actually a Master from a Coptic Temple, and after much discussion with Hamid's parents upon the Master's return, it was agreed that Hamid was to go into temple training. In Coptic temple training, Hamid was taught spiritual disciplines in emotional and mental control and meditation.

At age six, Hamid Bey was accepted by the Secret Temple Masters for special training. The Inner Temple of Learning was so far from his home that it took his mother and grandfather a week by donkey cart to arrive at their destination. Although homesick at first, the young boy knew it was a very special place of learning.

In this Inner School of Wisdom, each boy was taught to do everything he could to make life pleasant for the newcomer. No bragging or hazing was allowed. He experienced nothing but love and acceptance in the Temples. His teachers were kind and gentle, firm but always fair, and no fear or doubt was allowed to exist regarding his ability to accomplish his responsibilities.

The Temple Masters did not believe in putting a child into actual systematic training until age nine. In those early formative years, character was being developed, and careful records were kept of his progress. Personal health and private experiences were carefully directed by the teachers, who believed that whatever happened in the early upbringing of each child shaped permanent character. The brain being so sensitive, the slightest impression was deemed important. The avoidance of planting fear of any degree into a child's mind was emphasized. The child was shown the origination of fear and the means of overcoming all ramifications fear might create. Learning that fear dramatically affected delicate brain cells at a young age, and unless eliminated, fear in an uncontrolled state could create a habitual self-defensive attitude to manifest.

Human impulses toward selfishness, quarreling and all destructive tendencies were completely deleted from the temple boy in training. Hamid Bey's Master taught him as much about the influence of positivity in life as the boy could comprehend, creating situations that stimulated his susceptible brain, implanting mental impressions that molded his skills, his self-control, and dynamically active thought processes. Later in his training, he realized he was completely free of negative character traits and sub-conscious thought patterns.

His temple teachers thoroughly explained that the adult lifestyle was developed from habit patterns established during formative childhood years. One of his severest disciplines was to go out into the community and beg, learning by experience the attribute of humility and kindness in this realistic situation.

His first great lesson in the outer world was learning that the power of self-image is determined by how one is accepted in his environment. The Masters used practical methods of teaching by controlling the mind and emotions. The students were taught how to gain ultimate control of all facets of their nature. No attempt was exercised to make learning easy. No punishment for failure was permitted in school. Each student was allowed to explain his own reasoning and conduct. Total sympathy and respect were given to the student.

Routine exercises were practiced. Mundane tasks were made interesting and challenging. The children willingly and gladly worked after they understood the underlying purposes behind the assigned activities. Very early in the temple training, Hamid began to develop highly sensitized brain cells. The Masters knew intuitively the use of right and left brain activity, and taught advanced power of visualization to young and fertile minds.

At age nine, Hamid's body and mind were in perfect balance. It was at this age his temple training was accelerated. Now possessing a perfect physical body, his next task was to learn ultimate control by being taught to limit emotional and physical appetites. The mind was taught to be the most valuable mechanism to control. He learned how to use his mental faculties to fullest advantage. He began to understand in depth the true relationship between body and mind.

His first task was to develop and maintain a strong natural posture. Then he was given the understanding of the superconscious mind, the positive response of the body when quiet, then later taught how to concentrate on his breath and to attain maximum control of this natural process in perfect expression.

As Hamid grew in years, so did the advanced pace of his training. He was taught to place his body at the complete command of his will, and to enter into a state of suspended animation.

Perfect Balance Achieved

Hamid was continually shown the powerful potential of concentration in an extended series of temple lessons. At times when his body totally submitted to its master, the mind, complete comfort of body and peace of mind resulted. The body ceased to assert itself, leaving the individual free to identify itself with the object of concentration, which adequately prepared him for a deep meditative state.

Body mastery by thought control was accomplished by removing energy from emotion, nullifying sensation. He eventually mastered danger and fear and all negative emotions by completely withdrawing attention from them. This took sensation away from nerve endings, the nerves not reacting to external stimuli from the environment.

Students learned that the inner thinking process is accomplished by a well-known power called energy, more refined than electricity, but similar to magnetism. Our mental and emotional natures constantly produce and distribute this energy, capable of building and repairing the physical body.

Through certain knowledge of breathing techniques, trained Masters can positively utilize this energy from the atmosphere. Its essence is abundant, for it is known as the Breath of the Divine. The breath so long taken for granted has an infinite variety of secret purposes, applied to objectives known by the Masters. This manifested energy of breath obeys the laws of life building the body and then, when perfected, obeys the law of self-preservation by bringing invisible forces into the body as Pranic energy.

This advanced training of coordinated body and mind eventually permitted Hamid to inject long needles into his body without pain or bleeding. He possessed complete control over body sensations. It was ultimately under complete control of his will. This amazing body control was later documented by the American Medical Association when he obtained permanent residence in America.

The body, the spine, spinal cord, the nerve centers, and the relation of the spine were in total coordination with the brain. This developed body-mind control is presently unknown to the uninitiated, but this advanced knowledge has been known for centuries by the Masters. The posture practiced in meditation enabled a temple student to awaken his brain at instantaneous conscious command. Hamid was able to put his brain cells in a passive state at will, and being asleep in only one part of his mentality, he could still accomplish amazing feats in another remote part of the brain.

Hamid was given extensive training in transcending the laws of life and taught extensively how to use this ability to positive advantage for freedom of expression. So thoroughly was his training assimilated that he learned most of these lessons by the age of ten. He was given many lessons in emotional poise, the futility of anger, and giving no energy to negative emotions.

Every lesson was always followed by a a promise of more information—curiosity was never stifled—reasoning was a challenge to be constantly enjoyed. He learned many hidden multi-faceted selves existed within himself—each demanding expression and techniques on how to deal with them. He was taught truths regarding the motive of conduct being the basis of character, mental attitudes far more important than committing facts to memory. All learning is comparable to beads on a string, each fact a bead, each science a separate series of beads, but the string representing innate character.

When this reality is implanted in the formative years of childhood, stresses of life do not build, and the ability to control is accentuated. Early wisdom begets humility, a virtue wisely treasured, generating power, and setting into motion creative laws that bear fruit according to original motive.

Meditation in the Temple was practiced with daily regularity. Defined as controlled mental action, young Hamid searched within for greater understanding of the hidden mysteries. For the sincere and dedicated Temple pupil, progressive unfolding enabled the student to expand into wider realms of reality and finally tap into the inner universe. The ability to view the super physical worlds was gradually developed by dedicated practices. Each student eventually tapped higher realms extending beyond brain-mind memory.

Meditation awakened forgotten memory, enabling one to recall events in the experience of the soul of ages past. Recall assisted personal spirituality by revealing the universe and the relationship to all that is stored in the subconscious mind. Nothing is forgotten. When exercising the technique of recall, he knew he had been part of all creation. He began to revere being one with the All One. This feeling of becoming one with the All One is what Christ often referred to when He stated, "I and my Father are one."

Hamid Bey was taught to spontaneously enter a trance state—what physicians call catalepsy, or suspended animation. This permitted him to demonstrate—as he did for many years in Egypt and America—exceptional body and mind control by being buried alive for over 5,000 demonstrations without access to air for many hours.

Egyptian Masters

The Egyptian masters have adopted a method of inner plane communication that has existed for thousands of years. Wherever two Temple members were taught the technique, they used this telepathic procedure so effectively, information was transmitted on inner levels. In this extensive telepathic training, Hamid Bey progressed to the final Temple of Initiation.

Its history traces back 9,000 years. Very few know the temple's location, it being almost inaccessible. This has been necessary for the Coptic Templars, because throughout their history, they have been constantly persecuted. The Coptic Temple of Divine Wisdom is older than the Pyramid of Giza. This temple is a monument to the wisdom of the Atlanteans who migrated to Egypt from their sinking continent.

Their disciples have been taught the development of ultimate powers of mind and body preservation. During these 9,000 years, thirty Masters have served the temple, each one living an average lifespan of 300 years. The body of each Temple Master has been preserved by a secret process known to only the few. These Masters possess the secret of perpetual youth. The Law of Life declares they consciously make their ascension into higher realms when their work has been completed in this earth life.

Hamid's Final Training

Hamid's final training in the Temple of Triumph was completed at age eighteen years. His admonition from the Great Master was that the only value in time and eternity is one's own personal development and altruistic service. At his attained age of eighteen, he was initiated into the sacred mysteries of the White Brotherhood in the presence of his Master.

There were six preparatory temples of learning that Hamid passed through before he could enter the final temple, the Temple of Divine Wisdom. In order to get to this temple, it is necessary to swim the Nile and enter through a tunnel. The big test here is that the Nile is infested in this area with vast numbers of crocodiles. The only way to know whether crocodiles are in the murky water is to locate them by mind power.

In this temple, Hamid passed through the most challenging and final test. In the temple, a flower is cultivated which does not grow anywhere in the world except deepest central Africa. It is a beautiful white flower that gradually opens and closes. When open, the perfume of the flower is very pleasant, but is a deadly poison to humans. It is used to prove an initiate's physical and mental control.

The flower is placed in the center of a series of concentric circles. There are eleven circles in all; the eleventh one is closest to the flower. The initiate must keep his body independent of the poison, and sit for one hour in a circle, beginning with the outermost circle. Each circle moves the initiate closer to the flower and gives him one more ring. Hamid Bey made it to the seventh circle, which made him a seven-ring Master. The rings were symbolically worn on his headdress. When he attained the seventh degree, Hamid felt that he should leave the temple and go out into the world.

Hamid then went home to his family in Cairo, and shortly thereafter, served two years in World War I as an Air Force pilot. After his tenure in the service, he could not bring himself to go into the community business as offered by his father. His soul realized a more important destiny.

Houdini Challenged

In 1925, the famous magician Houdini had made many claims that his amazing feats could not be duplicated. The Egyptian Masters recognized this opportunity to demonstrate the power of Spirit operating through man. Utilizing their rare opportunity offered by Houdini, Hamid was sent to America in 1926 by his Temple Masters.

Three weeks after Hamid arrived, Houdini died. Hamid, then not knowing any English or any of the customs, signed up as a vaudeville act under a binding two-year contract. He spent the next two years, much to his disdain, doing his "act" on stage three times a day for sometimes heckling audiences.

After that experience, he became great friends with Paramahansa Yogananda and traveled with him doing shows and lectures together for many years, demonstrating universal laws of mind over matter. Hamid was the first Vice-President of Self-Realization Fellowship, the birth of Yoga. Paramahansa and Hamid were two of the greatest pioneers of metaphysics during the 1920's and 1930's.

Paramahansa Yogananda

Paramahansa Yogananda wrote the following tribute to Hamid Bey in the 1920's:

"Master Bey showed me that by touching anyone's wrist he could divine his thoughts. Each thought has a certain vibration and by contact with the pulse of the person thinking the thought, Master Bey receives the same vibration and consequently thinks the same thought. Later, he demonstrated to me his method of physical trance, in which he fell into my hands, breathless and almost lifeless. The stethoscope revealed that his heartbeat, at first fast, slowed down to an intermittent beat, and then got very slow.

"Master Bey can remain underground, buried for twenty-four hours, sealed in an air-tight casket, and can hold a thousand pounds on his chest. He controls his pulse at will—its beats appeared and completely disappeared at his will. He also pierces his body with long needles without bloodshed. The marks almost instantaneously disappeared after the needles were withdrawn. He thrusts these needles into his throat, cheeks, and tongue without pain. He can produce blood from one puncture and withhold blood from another. Most of these things he performed right in front of me. In the various cities where he visits, he often gives demonstrations before gatherings of eminent physicians and surgeons. In New York City, he submitted to burial for three hours. On this occasion, his body was sealed in a casket and placed six feet underground. The doctors who were present admitted that they could not explain the feat other than by Hamid Bey's declaration that by self-imposed catalepsy, he rendered his body almost lifeless.

"Passing needles through his cheeks and certain other of Master Bey's fat are performed, after long practice, by manipulating glands of the throat and by pressing certain nerves on the head. These are very interesting physiological phenomena showing that man can control the functions of the heart and all other organs of involuntary action. This is known to Hindu Yogis and Swamis who practice Yoga as well as to mystics of other sects."

Newspaper Reports

During Hamid Bey's public demonstrations, there were many types of reaction to his work. The following two newspaper accounts are representative of many reports by the news media during the 1920's and 1930's.

HAMID BEY, WONDER MAN, WHO ACCOMPLISHES WHAT SEEMS IMPOSSIBLE

Hamid Bey demonstrates his ability to withstand or not to feel pain; to control the heart and general circulation of the blood, preventing the flow of blood at will, and general catalepsy. He suits himself to the ordeal of being buried six feet under the ground for hours at a time, and is no worse for the experience as far as anyone can observe, and he himself says that it is good exercise and improves his health.

During these hours he does not appear to breathe at all. Concerning the control of the blood circulation, it is remarkable in that two or three medical men test his pulse, one at the heart itself, and the other two taking his pulse at both wrists. I have seen Hamid Bey, when under medial examinations by a committee, extend both arms and ask two of the physicians to examine the pulse at the right and left wrists respectively. At the same time, the third physician would take his heartbeat by means of a stethoscope. They would stand, watch in hand, and report their findings. At first all would report the same rate, say seventy-two to the minute, and then Hamid Bey would begin to concentrate. At the end of a minute the doctor holding the right wrist would report 64 to the minute, but the doctor holding the left wrist found 96 to the minute. The doctor listening to the heart would report 84 —and these were all at the same time! Now, this is something very remarkable. There is no doubt as to the facts. I have seen this demonstration many times, tested thoroughly by competent medical men. As soon as Hamid Bey ceases his concentration the pulse all over the body resumes its normal rate.

There is nothing essentially miraculous in this, but it is a remarkable demonstration of the control of the body by mental means, and has aroused the greatest interest wherever shown. It proves to us that this ability is the secret of his power to endure these long burials.

THE NEW YORK TIMES
January 21, 1927 • Page 36, Column 2

FAKIR BURIED HOURS, BEATS HOUDINI TIME

Hamid Bey Lies in Grave Nearly Three Hours to Explode the 'Shallow Breathing' Theory

FIVE FEET UNDER GROUND

Nose, Ears and Mouth Stuffed with Cotton—Curious Crowd at Englewood, N.J., Sees Test

Hamid Bey, youngest of the Egyptian fakirs, stood before a damp open grave in the front yard of Walter A. Shannon's home in Englewood, N.J., at 1 o'clock yesterday afternoon. Around him pushed a curious crowd of men, women, children, dogs, and six gravediggers waiting to bury him for three hours. A fine rain fell on the Bey's white gandourah head-dress and flowing mantle; and his ankles above a pair of inadequate-looking sandals, were exposed to the cold.

Beside the Bey stood two henchmen, Zulicfer Effendi, whose white robe was topped off with a cerise gandourah and a purple umbrella, announced that Hamid would forthwith explode the late Harry Houdini's theory that the burial of fakirs was accomplished through "shallow breathing" of a limited amount of air rather than by the aid of self-willed catalepsy.

Goes into Cataleptic State

The skeptical crowd surged closer as the moment for burial approached. Then at 1:10 o'clock the Bey made a gasping sound and stiffened out in the cataleptic state. Two doctors, Francis P. Weston of New York and William Silverstein of Newark, aided by three newspaper men, stuffed the ears, nose and mouth of the fakir with cotton, and he was forthwith laid five feet below the level of the lawn in a narrow inner grave. A little sand was heaped over his face, and boards were placed over the inner hole. This left as much air as Houdini had in his steel casket when, last Summer, he was lowered into the Hotel Shelton pool in New York. To cap the performance, the gravediggers then get to it to fill in the three-foot hole above the inner grave. With this accomplished, the Bey was abandoned for three hours minus eight minutes by all save his henchmen. They took turns sitting at the grave's head on an old kitchen chair, waiting for the signal from the electric bell that might signify Hamid was in trouble.

And the mixed, inquisitive crowd all went to Walter Shannon's home to eat the sandwiches and drink the coffee provided by his wife, the former Leona Le Marr, "the girl with the thousand eyes." Under the emporary [sic] spell of the Orient they sat around discussing such subjects as "after all, life is an indefinite thing."

Betters Houdini Record

The first hour went by and then the second. The fakir was still underground. He had passed the record of Rahman Bey, who had been placed in an immersion casket in the Hudson for an hour. And he had gone beyond the record of Houdini, who had, by shallow breathing, remained in a casket in the Shelton pool for an hour and a half.

Near 4 o'clock, however, the three Irish gravediggers began to uncover the fakir. The three negro gravediggers stood by ready to "spell" their companions. Shortly after 4 Hamid was lifted from the position he had occupied for nearly three hours. The cotton was still in his mouth, nose and ears. The dirt had been undisturbed since they had showered it over his face.

Once in the air, the Egyptian shivered and gradually came to life. He murmured one word, "Houdini," and broke into a broad grin. Afterward he said he had communed with Houdini, but refused to report the conversation. His pulse and respiration, which had been 72 and 18 respectively before burial, were the same after coming out of the cataleptic state, according to the two doctors. Houdini's pulse, after the "shallow breathing," registered 142.

Zulicfer said he had been in communication with Hamid all the time the latter was underground. Asked at specific intervals how his protégé was getting along, he would reply: "Il est bien."

Terry Turner of Loew's, Inc., who arranged the performance, said he didn't know about giving the fakir a vaudeville contract. "The audience would walk out before three hours are up," he said. Elated by his victory, the Bey said he would perform the same stunt soon "for three days."

Painless Piercings

Another demonstration which Hamid Bey gives of his unique powers is permitting the flesh or tissues of the body to be pierced with long pins or daggers, seemingly without pain.

For the purpose, long hat pins are usually used. These are pushed through the cheeks, breasts, arms, or shoulders. There is no doubt but that the pins are actually inserted. It is Hamid Bey's practice to walk among his audiences with the pins sticking into or through him as I have described. If any skeptic is present, he is usually allowed to insert the pins himself. There is no preparation of the skin with drugs, previous piercings, or anything of the sort. Physicians who perform the tests have examined the area of the skin before and afterward, choosing the particular spot involved, inserting and extracting the pins. There is no trick whatsoever involved in the demonstration. At the conclusion of the experiment the pins are withdrawn and only pink holes mark the spot where they have been inserted.

Hamid Bey will ask where it is desired that blood shall flow from the wounds, and he permits it to flow—or refuses —at will. Sometimes he will permit blood to flow from two of the holes, and refuse it from the other two.

During one of the television shows of Ed Sullivan, a very well-known TV host in the 50's and 60's, Hamid Bey was a guest on his show. During the show, Hamid Bey laid on a bed of nails and Ed Sullivan, who weighed over 200 pounds, stood on his chest in front of a nation-wide audience. He took off his shirt and you couldn't even see where the nails had penetrated his skin.

Voluntary Body Catalepsy

However, his demonstration of body catalepsy is the most remarkable of all. His body becomes rigid, the pulse becomes almost imperceptible, and respiration apparently ceases entirely. Consciousness is said to be obliterated, and nothing is remembered of the time spent in that state. In this mental state, Hamid Bey permits himself to be buried underground, with or without coffin, and is revived at the end of that time.

I have watched this experiment when a committee of disinterested, local men chose the spot, so that secret air tubes, tunnels for possible escape and the like were impossible. At one time, on a cold and rainy day, the ice had to be broken on the ground before the digging began. The earth was undisturbed at the end of the burial.

It was the unanimous verdict of the medical committee and newspapermen present on that day that no fraud was possible, and they so stated in the public press on the following morning. Medical men say that the cataleptic condition is a real physical and mental state, and that it cannot be artificially imitated. They say that during catalepsy the pulse seems entirely suspended and that the subject ceases perceptible breathing.

On one occasion when Hamid Bey had undergone the burial test, at its conclusion the pulse could not be detected. When he came out of the cataleptic state the heartbeat jumped to 120, then fell to 84.

Another peculiarity about this man is that when he is buried on a hot day in a sealed casket, he comes out without perspiration on his body, while those who are about him and functioning normally are dripping with perspiration. This fact alone should prove that the state is unique and genuine.

On the other hand, Hamid Bey can be buried in the ice cold ground for three hours without ill effects whatsoever.

Imitations Possible?

It is true that these long burials can be imitated, but the conditions involved are invariably different from those prevailing at a genuine burial. Sometimes oxygen tanks are smuggled into a coffin or a tube is connected with the box under cover of clothing. But in all the public or test burials of Hamid Bey none of these conditions have prevailed.

Some performers have tried to duplicate this by simply remaining in a coffin as long as possible, and emerging when life could no longer be sustained. Such was the demonstration given by the late Harry Houdini. Houdini was submerged in a metal coffin for about an hour and a half. But when he emerged he was deathly white, running with perspiration, and with a pulse of 142. It is the opinion of those who watched Houdini attempt to duplicate, by mechanical means, the feats of these Eastern adepts, that his life was appreciably shortened by the terrific strain.

Different When Genuine

But where the feat is genuine, there is no evidence of strain, or in fact, of any unfavorable physical effect. It becomes evident to a competent and careful observer that the inner states are entirely dissimilar.

The state of self-imposed catalepsy is most interesting to observe. He stands erect, presses strongly on his forehead with his fingers and then on his throat with his thumbs. A few seconds later he throws his head back with gasping intake of breath, the body perfectly rigid, and is caught by his assistants, who immediately place him in the coffin. He remains in this state of rigidity throughout the burial. At its conclusion, the body is raised to an upright position by attendants, the hands are forcefully pulled away from the face and neck, and with a sudden rush of air from the lungs the body collapses, being sustained by two attendants. The breathing and pulse slowly return, and in about five minutes he is himself again.

So far as I have observed, there are certain specific physical and mental requirements to enter the cataleptic state voluntarily, and I think that it requires long years of practice and development of a most unusual kind to accomplish the feat successfully and safely.

A True Master

Hamid Bey exemplified the personification of the word Master. The Masters of Egyptian Temples are scientific in their work, accumulating conclusively tested facts for centuries. When a sufficient number of facts are substantiated, giving evidence of stability of law, organized facts become a science.

The Western world follows this same procedure. A major basic difference is that Masters express the greatest service possible on this planet in the form of personal unfoldment, and the study of human nature. Masters declare all inventions secondary to humanity's manifold expression. To them, such discoveries only have value as they influence mankind to awaken their latent personal powers. Western twentieth century society is just beginning to accept this philosophy that Egyptian masters have practiced for thousands of years.

Masters are scientists, artisans, mechanics, and philosophers. They believe in diligent work and take pride in teaching meaningful services in developing successful habit patterns in the lives of their students. They consider nature the handiwork of the one Creative Principle, the passive or nurturing half of creation, rightfully called "Mother," the feminine principle.

God is the positive pole which originally created substance, power, and purpose manifested in nature—everything that comes within our range of observation, visible and invisible. The sum of this acquired knowledge and wisdom constitutes Coptic Philosophy.

To maintain his temple rank of seven-ring Master, Hamid had to return to Egypt every seven years and go through additional tests and examinations by his Master. In 1936, Hamid returned to Egypt and had a great spiritual experience. He was taken astrally by his Master to the secret Archive Chamber of the Great Pyramid. Hamid's true mission in the United States was revealed to him. The United States was to become the new Holy Land, and the Coptic Order would be established here. In 1937, Master Hamid Bey founded the Coptic Fellowship in Los Angeles, California.

My Experiences with Hamid Bey

Master Hamid Bey was the greatest man I have ever known. I had the honor of personally seeing him in a variety of life roles, including being a loving husband, father, grandfather, boatman, golfer, friend, and mentor. He exemplified the highest ideals of successful living by demonstrating self-mastery skills in a dramatic spiritual way.

He is also one of the most prolific metaphysical writers in history. And while The Power of Your Mind Versus Fear was originally written in the 1950's, this powerful book contains ideas that can help anyone break loose from the fear that abounds in our "modern" age.

In the 1970's, I was playing golf with Master Hamid Bey in California. He was not a particularly great golfer, but he was very enthusiastic about the game. When we reached the back nine of the golf course, he hit the ball and it landed about 25 yards in front of the stream running through the course. He was not playing well that day and I expected him to knock the ball into the water.

He dubbed the shot (hit a poor shot that never left the ground). It was headed toward the stream and I thought it destined to go into the water. However, there was a very tiny bridge going across the river, and his ball hit that bridge and it went across the stream. I was immediately in shock, and yelled at him, "That was fantastic, Great Master! How did you do that?"

He ignored me, and would not look at me or address the subject at all. So I thought he was showing his usual state of humility (and teaching me the lesson of humility) because I witnessed a magnificent miracle that day. Two holes later we again came upon the stream and he was in a similar position—25-50 yards in front of the stream. He again dubbed his shot, and it was going into the stream—except a duck walked across in front of the stream, and the ball hit the duck, which prevented the ball from going into the stream. At this time I was even more excited to say, "Master, you've done this twice in three holes! What a great miracle!" He did not respond to the subject after the round at all.

On a personal level, this is one of the greatest miracles I have ever witnessed in my life.

Prediction of Marriage

Here's another example of Hamid Bey's mastery.

At one point, I had decided I was not going to get married. I was satisfied being a single man and continue with that philosophy.

Hamid Bey visited the Coptic Center in Detroit in April of 1970. Master Stanley, who was my mentor and teacher, had a secretary who came down from the office, and said that Master Bey wanted to talk to me. I went up, and Hamid Bey greeted me and said, "I have some news for you. You're going to meet your wife in two months."

I said, "But Master, I've decided I'm not going to get married."

He said, "You're still going to meet her in two months."

I played in a golf tournament in June of 1970 and I needed a date for the banquet. A friend referred a woman named Nancy for a possible date, and I called her to go with me. Nancy worked in his office. When I called her, I was not impressed with what I heard over the telephone. However, I did make the date with her.

During the tournament, my partner and I were winning the first two matches, but losing the third round. I said that if we didn't win, I wasn't going out with Nancy. The bottom line is we did miraculously win the tournament, and I did meet my wife in two months. In June of 1970, Hamid Bey's prophecy was fulfilled.

Service to Others

Hamid Bey's life was dedicated to the service of others. He conducted weekly self-mastery training classes in Los Angeles after he founded the Coptic Fellowship of America on April 28, 1937. He wrote 345 Egyptian Mystery School lessons that will be promoted nationally over the next few years. He also published My Experiences Preceding 5000 Burials in 1938.

Tenets of the Christian Masters were delivered in lectures, study courses, workshops, and simple talks to Coptic students by Hamid Bey and Kurt Stanley, U.S. Midwest Coptic Director for many years, who shared their wisdom with the Coptic members from the mid-thirties to the mid-seventies. Their students cherished their humility and dedication to the preservation of The Word.

Master Bey passed away on July 16, 1976. His teachings of the ancient lineage of the White Brotherhood Essene Heritage and Egyptian Coptic self-mastery training are being taught at the Coptic Center in Grand Rapids, Michigan, and at conferences throughout the United States.

Before his passing on July 16, 1976, when Hamid's soul consciously exited his physical body by consciously lowering the blood flow, he transferred to the Coptic students the knowledge that had been preserved since it had been passed on to him from his Temple Masters.

Section 4:
Sparks of Light

Planetary Numerology

Einstein evolved no new theory when he presented his thesis of the Absolute and the Relative to the world.

He did, however, give what is called scientific sanction to the philosopher's dictum. He measured the measureless and weighed the weightless. He counted out in terms of algebraic formulae with mathematical precision, a mathematical definition of the Absolute and Relative.

The scientific world acclaimed the new hero as a discoverer of a new idea. Yet, ages ago, the Egyptians built their temples, the pyramids, and wrote their hieroglyphics with equal or superior knowledge of these identical facts.

Origins

It has been said that the teachings originated with the Spiritual Hierarchy of our Solar System and were introduced to Earth during the time of the Lemurian civilization and later given to the Atlanteans.

After the destruction of Atlantis, schools were established in Egypt by the survivors to carry on their sacred traditions. Inherited from the Atlantean Mystery Schools, Hebrew—a form of ancient Gaelic which carried mystery keys—was the sacred tongue of the Egyptian Mystery Schools. These keys are a system of numerical values assigned to the letters of the Hebrew language. This alphanumeric system was probably the model for Pythagoras' own system of numerology.

Pythagoras wasn't the only Greek to influence higher learning in the ancient world. Hermes, believed to have been a man who was later deified, preceded Pythagoras by several thousand years. He was responsible for giving mankind the arts and sciences known as mathematics, chemistry, law, philosophy, geography, magic, and astrology, among others. Hermes was known to the Egyptians as "Thoth," to the Jews as "Enoch," and to the Latins as "Mercury."

The Book of Thoth was a volume of sacred teachings and its pages consisted of symbols and hieroglyphics which were purported to endow the initiated with great powers over the elements. A great deal of evidence exists that supports the claim of the ancient teachings that The Book of Thoth is the Tarot, the set of 78 cards of divination which has been preserved by the gypsies, who are believed to have descended from the bloodline of the ancient Egyptian priests.

It was within the Mystery Schools of Egypt where Pythagoras and many of his contemporaries—as well as other well-known initiates throughout our planet's history (Jesus was initiated in the Great Pyramid at Giza)—chose to preserve their higher teachings through the use of coded language.

Egyptian Universal Principle

"I am the Alpha and the Omega, the beginning and the end." In these words are encompassed, then, the "All in All." The Egyptian teachers gave the entire significance of their teaching to comprehension of this Universal Principle. It was called "Amen" or the "Hidden One." To ancient Egyptians it meant Foundation as the essence from whence all is manifested.

The ideograph accompanying this essence is composed of the ancient Egyptian phonetic sounds A-M-N, constituting the word AMEN and pronounced AWMEN.

The first character is the closed elongated square-rectangle from which springs the mystical number seven, denoting completion. From the earliest period of antiquity up to the present time, this has been a sacred and mystical number. We note some of the instances in the Bible—the seven days of creation and rest; the seven fat and seven lean; seven years of service which Jacob served for his coveted Rachel only to get her sister; the seven churches and seven candlesticks of Revelations, each of which denotes the end of a period, completion, unity.

The letter 'M', being the 13th letter of the alphabet, symbolizes power, the power of the one, of unity.

The character representing N (en) is a series of opposing crossed lines. This, of course, represents the rebirths and yet one, life, unity.

The AMEN as a whole is intended to convey the idea of the conclusion, the ultimate, the whole, one, unity.

That Which Cannot Be Separated

This same idea is also contained within the meaning of individual itself—a concept-word consisting of IN – meaning not, and DIVIDO – meaning divided. That which cannot be divided.

This is true both of individual human and individual objects, that which cannot be divided or separated from the One Truth. It does not mean that Hu-man cannot be dissected, for the individual can be. If this be done, we should observe lungs, liver, heart, brain, bones, and nerves; yet the composite is an individual. Each of the members is an expression, point, in a type-line. This line is undivided and unbroken in all nature, all the universe. There is a relationship of every center to a corresponding center as, for example, a planet in the universal whole.

We have started on the road to make important discoveries of a universal nature. It causes us to contemplate the idea of an undivided universe, bound together by invisible lines of force, each line independent of the other lines, but interrelated in action, all converging to a common center, the Hidden One. We suggest to ourselves that each nerve in our body fulfills a definite function individual in its action but interrelated, converging to a common center, the nerve center of that function, and finally to the brain, the Amen of all these centers.

Upon such a foundation we can account for the entire forces operating to continue the process of evolution and, human destiny included, as part and parcel of its action therein; to think in lesser terms divides the universe into duality. This is unthinkable from any truly scientific basis.

The very term, Universe, itself, denies it, for the word means UNI – One and VERSE – Truth. One truth, reality. One truth, the all-inclusive, One truth, with many forms of manifestation. One truth, Godman and Godwoman. We unite the cause and the effect into Godpersons, for cause and effect are one.

Creation of the Universe

Let us now look upon this foundation by viewing the structures which have been built upon it.

Let us look at the glory of the Heavens, the wonders of the world and humankind. We discover from this survey a unitary plan running through it all and becoming all.

Many theories have been advanced as to the way of the Creation. Among these is the Nebular hypothesis. According to this theory, the Universe was of one substance alone, a gaseous substance pervading all space. By reason of movement within itself—a rotary motion, a whirling of the mass took place. The centrifugal force caused condensation of the gases at the center of the mass. Heat thus generated fired the gases at the center, and a Sun was born. The force of the same movement now began throwing off huge masses due to irregularity of the form of the Sun. These masses in turn continued to rotate worlds in themselves. Through the Law of Attraction and Repulsion, certain of these collected in a system, controlled by individualized laws peculiar to their position relative to the entire whole.

Among these groups was our Solar System with its center, the Sun, and with nine sister planets to the Earth. These planets cast forth from the Sun, condensed to matter, also hurled from themselves huge masses. This was the natural action necessary to assume a globular form to match the general shape running throughout the Universe—the circle. These cast-off masses became the moons accompanying the planets.

As these masses cooled, the atmosphere around them became gaseous envelopes condensing into water, a combination of gases necessary to the conditions of life. Among these planets of our system, the Earth has all the potentials of life. The Earth has all the conditions necessary for manifestation of the varied forms which now exist, while it is probable the other planets have not, at least as far as life as we know it is concerned. This theory extended to inanimate life on the Earth, giving a real basis upon which the theory of physical evolution can be acceptable. The same can be said of the theory of the Vortex Rings, a more modern, but less wisely accepted, theory.

Universal philosophy comprehends a self-existent intelligence in operation, itself becoming, through processes described, the very substance of its creation.

Symbologies of Number 13

Planetary numerology reveals much of what we need to bring about true peace on Earth. One of the more important numbers related to our topic is the number 13.

1. Twelve forces grouped in a circle around one force form a powerful unity vibrating to 13. Herein lies the secret of plenty, peace and power for personal and planetary welfare.

2. In the formula of 13 is found the key to the words, "Where two or three are gathered together in my name, there am I in the midst of them." Through the right and proper assemblage of the forces of 12 and 1 (13), "All forces of love are given unto you for the benefit of all." The two, the inner and outer, spirit and matter, are as one. Full union of an individual with their higher self is where we become the Light of the World.

3. In the Hall of Accomplishment are 13 chairs. Above each chair is a shield symbolizing the deeds performed by the one individual proved worthy to sit in that #13 seat. #13 synthesizes the forces of the 1 surrounded by 12.

4. Mem is the 13th letter of the Hebrew alphabet, representing the feminine Mother mystery. Processes of the Mother mystery symbolize birth, sublimation, and transfiguration. The Biblical Book of Revelation is keyed to #13 completion of the feminine fourfold process (birth, sublimation, and transfiguration), consummation of the magical power of #13 depicting the vision of the woman clothed with the Sun.

5. "And there appeared a great wonder in Heaven, a woman clothed with the Sun, the moon under her feet, and upon her head a crown of twelve stars." Revelation 12:1.

6. Each star of the twelve on her crown symbolizes one sign of the zodiac and the fulfilling of the requirements,

responsibilities, and attainment of power of each zodiac sign. The "moon under her feet" represents the subconscious mind which is now under control and the unlimited potential of the subconscious reservoir is available for tapping its infinite reserves.

7. The 13th letter Mem is the most significant of the three mother letters. It is ranked second in power only to the (1) of absolute Unity. The form of the letter Mem is similar to the Aquarius sign symbol: the shepherd of the skies pouring water that bears 13 stars on to earth.

8. The use of 13 in the Seal of the U.S.A. is in direct obedience to law and order as required by its destiny. 13 means either death through failure and degeneration or ultimate attainment and complete regeneration of the New Order of the Ages. No halfway measure exists with 13. It demands all or nothing. 13 truly signifies death if old habitual ways of living are continued or a true state of transfiguration if the new is adopted and manifested.

Numerology of 2012

The year 2012 is a very interesting analogy for the planet. We have to remove the zero in 2012 to find out what 212 means in planetary numerology terms. First of all, 212 degrees is the boiling point. We light workers affirm that the boiling point will create a positive future for planet Earth. Win-win for the peoples of all religions and nations. Remember, all children are our children. The future always depends on the attitude of world servers who are dedicated to creating a positive future for all of humanity. If political leaders acknowledge that all nations are their symbolic brothers and sisters, we have a win-win- situation. If part of our daily prayers involve the vision of international political leaders not ever using the option of W.A.R., we have a winner. If political leaders acknowledge that "Thou shalt not kill" is one of the Ten Commandments to be followed to the letter, we have another winner.

Most countries outside of the U.S. do not acknowledge that women are equal to men. This concept is totally not true. So, another one of our daily prayers should be that politicians give equal rights to women in their country; that women and men are equal, creating a prototype for other countries to emulate.

The year 2012 has another interpretation without the zero. #212 is also the birthday of Abraham Lincoln. This powerful symbology is so important to our planetary future.

Just think of all the positive values that Lincoln possessed during his lifetime. Freedom and equal rights for all people are the first two of the foundations he created for the future of humanity.

As Jesus proclaimed during his lifetime, "Greater things I do, ye shall do." Lincoln continued this theme with his dedication to equal rights for women and men, plus the equality of all races, to eventually manifest into the round table of nations in a scenario where all nations share natural resources and will help all other nations to attain greatness on all levels.

A major discovery this year has created a new revelation of the prophesied 2012 prophecy Every person on Earth born between the time period of January 1, 1900, and December 31, 1999, has exactly the same power number—111. This is a significant discovery because of the obvious earth changes going on before our eyes.

To prove the validity of this 111 theory, add the last two years of the year you were born to your age on your birthday in 2011. You will find that total will be 111. All we have to do is analyze the timing of the interpretation of

111 to understand its tremendous impact on our planetary future.

Let's begin by going back to the most important presidential address in our country's history, the Gettysburg Address. The date Mr. Lincoln chose to make this important address for freedom of all peoples was November 19, 1863.

Aquarius symbolizes the power of thought and prayer. Simply stated, if each of us utilizes the power of thought and prayer every day from now into the future, the Earth will be positively changed. On all levels (physical, mental, and emotional), the future symbolizes springtime and each of us in our minds plant powerful positive mental seeds into the world dimensions to take our rightful position of co-creators. Prayers by many will change Earth's future conditions because of its springtime planetary significance for a positive planetary tomorrow.

Decoding Revelation

It is the probable misapplication of these teachings which is responsible of the misinterpretation of the Book of Revelation. Indeed, its very authorship has been in question for nearly 1800 years.

Manly P. Hall, in his *Secret Teachings of All Ages*, states that the authorship of the controversial Book of Revelation—regarded as an enigmatic example of Gnostic Christian writings—has been a matter of dispute since the second century A. D. That dispute raged on for centuries and included, in the third century, Dionysius of Alexandria and his contemporary, Eusebius, who wrote under the name John the Divine.

It has also been suggested that, owing to the contents of the Book of Revelation, it bears all the earmarks of pagan theology, which is additional evidence that its author was probably schooled in the mystery tradition.

The subject of Biblical prophecy has been a difficult issue for theologians, Biblical scholars, and modern-day seers to resolve. This is as much due to the enigmatic nature of prophetic writings as to obvious differences in belief systems. Even those who prefer to interpret prophecy literally will concede that some symbolism is intermingled with what they believe is fact.

The Book of Revelation is probably the most heavily debated book of the Bible. The identity of its author is a minor issue when we consider that the literal interpretation of the horrific scenes described in Revelation's twenty-two chapters has been such a great perpetrator of fear, our greatest enemy. It is precisely these fear-based interpretations which I intend to defuse, for we must conquer our fear if we are to realize our full potential as a people.

To fully understand the premise set forth in these pages, an understanding is required of the manner in which the Bible has been altered over the past 2000 years. Coptic minister, Martin Anderson, provides some insight into this subject:

"After Moses received the Secret Doctrine, he proved his secret order of Essenes among his elect of Israelites. The secret order of Essenes kept the wisdom pure throughout the Aryan Age until the time of the Messiah, Jesus Christ. . .

"The Essenes called all their literature the Book of Enoch (named after Enoch, an ancestor of Noah, and an Atlantean initiate). . .The Book of Enoch predates Christianity by thousands of years. . (and) parallels the Book of Revelation and Genesis, and there are indications that the Book of Enoch may have been the style manual for these first and last books of the Bible . . .

"It was at the end of the Fifth Century A. D. that the Church decided to replace the Book of Enoch with the Book of Revelation, because (it was believed) John wrote the Revelation and it fitted the mystical charismatic image the Church was creating for Jesus. The Book of Enoch did not fit into the political policies of the Church of that day. . .The reason apparent for withdrawing the Book of Enoch was that it pointed to pre-Christian beginnings of the doctrine upon which Christianity is based."

Historically, there is a great deal of evidence that the Bible as a whole was tampered with at different times to suit the purposes of the Church authorities.   They are not initiated into the Mysteries, and therefore would not have understood the hidden meanings or higher purpose of the coded texts which served as a basis for Biblical scripture. Many are the critics who decry the rewriting of the Bible which has muddied the waters of knowledge concerning the true document.

World Changes Predicted

The subject of world changes has been receiving a great deal of attention as so much has been prophesied about events that are to occur as we enter a new millennium. This is not a new phenomenon by any means.   Every one thousand years, a whole rash of millennial prophecies are reported as the human psyche anticipates the birth of a new era in human life on this planet. New interpretations of Biblical prophecy emerge in tandem with new visions from contemporary seers. Add to this the fuel of increasingly frequent natural catastrophes and you have a fertile seedbed for the incubation of "millennial fever."

Of the more compelling prophetic offerings, one that holds a great deal of promise is a code recently discovered in the Bible by Dr. Eliyahu Rips, an Israeli mathematician.

Dr. Rips' discovery has passed the stringent tests of peer review and confirmation by a high-level code breaker in the U.S. National Security Agency.

The code is only found in the Hebrew version of the Bible but has been found to be highly accurate in describing events that have occurred and, more importantly, will occur, if the prophecies are fulfilled. The details of the code itself are complicated, but in simple terms it consists of a "skip-sequencing" method of locating letters to find a hidden word or words.

This code was discovered with a computer program written specifically for this task and has revealed 3000-year old prophecies that have been fulfilled, such as the assassination of Yitzhak Rabin, the elections of President Clinton and Prime Minister Netanyahu, the Oklahoma City bombing, as well as the Kobe, Japan, earthquake. The code also has revealed that we can prevent such devastating events as a world-wide holocaust for within a key section of the Hebrew text it gives the phrase, "Will you change" in conjunction with the words, "Holocaust of Israel" and "You delayed," as well as the years 1996 and 2000.

Author Drosnin believes that these encodings reflect probabilities that exist and that the outcome—whether positive or negative—depends upon our own actions. As the code is further studied, I would hope that the researchers would focus upon positive events to give people the opportunity to see what our other options are and how we can prevent further global destruction and turmoil.

The Light of the World

As a planetary numerologist, I'm often analyzing the numbers associated with dates, events, and ideas. The most powerful numbers I've ever encountered are found in the phrase, "Light of the World," which embodies the same energy as December 21, 2012, the end of the Mayan calendar.

In planetary numerology, there are many different ways to analyze numbers. While this is a vast and interesting topic, it's also outside the scope of this book. However, in using the Star of David pattern, this phrase (Light of the World) leads to becoming a co-creator.

Further analysis reveals that those of us who consider ourselves lightworkers and wish to bring light and hope to the world must accept the responsibility to become God Conscious.

The goal of this book is to give you the tools you need to become both a Light of the World and God Conscious.

Where Prophesies Come From

Other sources of prophecy also focus on the negative, although there are those which focus on the positive, also. It all depends upon where the attention is focused. After all, prophecy is merely the prediction of a possible event and not set in stone.

From where do prophecies come? Prophets, ancient and modern, acquire their visions in various means from the great data bank of the Cosmos, the Akashic Records or what Jung called the collective unconscious.

What is often not understood, however, is that what they are perceiving are probabilities which exist in a sort of existential limbo, an alternate universe where events only emerge into our physical reality if the conditions are right.

In other words, the likelihood of an event occurring depends upon certain conditions being met, and those conditions are the result of decisions and choices we make individually and collectively.

Therefore, if we understand that our choices determine the reality we experience, we can change the nature of our future experience by altering the nature of our choices. If we choose to live together in peace, accept all people as our sisters and brothers, honor the Earth, and work together to make the world a better place for all people, we can avert the disastrous events that have been prophesied.

Some of our most illustrious prophets have said the same thing. Nostradamus, Edgar Cayce, and the Hopi prophecies, in spite of the fact that they have seen tremendous destruction in their visions, have all stated that we can avert these disasters by changing our behavior and priorities. All have called for a more spiritual focus to counteract the negative effects of our past actions. After all, this is the purpose of prophecy, to give humanity a chance to alter its future. Three principles of prophecy are the foundation for this statement:

1. A negative prophecy fulfilled is a prophecy failed.
2. Any event that has not yet happened can be prevented.
3. Achieving a positive end result is the true purpose of prophecy.

Symbolism

Symbolism is a universal language. It speaks to us in the mystic realms where archetypes don the costumes of our common human attributes, and myths are acted out on the stage of the collective unconscious. Symbols are present everywhere in our lives; indeed, the letters which form our written language are themselves symbols.

The ancients understood the power of symbols and that they were essentially representative of the higher spiritual principles which gave them form. To both preserve for posterity and conceal the sacred Mysteries from the uninitiated, the guardians of divine knowledge went to great lengths to symbolically encode higher truths in their writings and mythologies.

While human cognitive powers are limited by perception, the unconscious mind has no limits to its comprehension, and it is to this mind that these symbologies speak.

The great ages of antiquity hid this divine knowledge in elaborate stone sculptures and artwork, the measurements of monumental buildings and mathematical formulae, and in their mythological stories and sacred texts. These truths were carefully preserved to ensure that humankind would not lose its access to the divine laws.

Comprehension of these divine laws is essential to the reawakening of the slumbering spirit within the human form, a matter which was of supreme importance to the ancient mystics as it is to mystics of today.

The illumined Masters kept their secrets hidden and preserved through the establishment of the Mystery Schools. There existed many mystery schools in ancient times, all of which required initiation and a devotion to secrecy. Their teachings have been preserved through the writings of such great thinkers as Pythagoras and Plato, both of whom were criticized for revealing the secret teachings to the uninitiated.

While both philosophers studied at many centers of higher learning, they were greatly influenced by the teachings of Orpheus, who had been initiated into the Egyptian Mysteries. Pythagoras—himself an initiate in the Egyptian Mysteries and perhaps most well known for his work in mathematics—was also influenced by the Babylonian and Chaldean Mysteries. For our purposes we will focus on the Egyptian Mystery tradition, for it is from here that our Western traditions evolved.

United States Taking Incentive

Of the Western traditions, the United States seems to be one country taking the initiative, though there are many light groups in many other nations. To succeed, the movement must be worldwide; the heritage of America has always been freedom from want and fear, and the right to make personal choices. Sometimes it drifts away from these basic concepts, but the ship of state has a way of righting itself. The heritage goes deep.

The Hierarchy that established the United States in 1776 implanted in people's minds the gifts of the Ages.

The Great Seal of the United States is a symbol brought forth by the Hierarchy, which other nations should aspire to in terms of human dignity and freedom.

Masters oversaw the organizational work of the U.S. Constitution and Bill of Rights, and reincarnated to walk among people to get the job done. The ascended master St. Germaine was very instrumental in the construction of the U.S. Government.

The New Israel

In this new civilization, centered in the United States of America—the New Israel—we shall see a truer, more positive-oriented schooling for the young, and a wider, greater understanding of the Divine by all social classes.

A harmonious welding of the religious and the scientific communities into one great philosophy of mutual understanding and respect for the principles of each will occur, bringing together the wonders of laboratories and the truths of the Cosmos. All humanity will be taught to enjoy a new life of greater mind and less physical developments.

In the New World, more than anywhere else on this earth plane, all races and nationalities of the Earth are blended together. Out of this blend shall spring the highly evolved man and woman of tomorrow. Indeed, a mental and physical superman and superwoman—a race that by its universally strong faith in the Supreme Wisdom shall create a civilization the equal of none that ever existed before on this planet.

The country of America has been chosen as the New Israel, for this is where the birth of freedom occurred.

It is also comprised of the nationalities of all countries. Diversified Americans are willing to learn and not be tied down by heavy tradition.

The trend of divine illumination has always moved from east to west. The first Christian order of things was the Coptic in Egypt. From the Coptic was born the Greek Orthodox Church and the Roman Catholic Church.

So THE WORD invaded the Coptic Church religion instituted during the life of Jesus the Christ, then moved from Egypt to Greece and Rome. From Greece, it moved into the Asiatic Countries, including Russia. From Rome, it moved into Central Europe and England.

Suffering the Christian dispensation—the Inquisition during the years of the Middle Ages—the church divided into Catholic and Protestant. Leaders such as Martin Luther protested and created their own blend of Christianity, which subsequently divided and re-divided. Now we are a Christian divided church.

The more substance is divided, the weaker it becomes. Religion has become subjugated to politics, to materialism, and to militarism. We are in strife because we have not practiced the precepts of Jesus the Christ. Unity in diversity will again triumph as we begin to expend energy to unify our efforts.

Armistice Day

November 11, 1949. The spiritual symbology has great meaning.

1949 – (49.) 7 x 7 equals 49. The 11th of November, again the number 11, the eleventh month, the 11th hour of the Egyptian philosophy when the human body has reached its smallest shadow. On the 12th hour, the soul will be able to depart from the human body because there is no longer a shadow. The 12th hour is the hour of transition, when the soul has no more need for the body, and the ego of man and has selfless desires to fulfill. The soul is now given the Egyptian wings, and can fly into eternity. It is freed from the bondage of physical existence.

The 11th of November is also the day of peace—Armistice Day. A coincidence—the 11th day, the 11th hour, 1949?

The U.S. has adopted a seal, and on one side of this seal is a pyramid. The pyramid was created and designed purposely. Whether the designer realized the purpose on the conscious level, God knew and worked through this individual who adapted this seal. 48 stones. The 49th is the golden cap—the all-seeing spiritual eye.

Stars and Stripes

It is clear from the symbolism in our national icons, including those depicted on our one-dollar bill, that the United States of America was founded on spiritual principles. The stated purpose was to create "a government of the people, by the people, and for the people."

On a deeper level, there existed a planetary vision for democracy, even though it has not been without its dark moments. We can cite the horrendous crimes committed against the native people who originally inhabited the North American continent as an example.

Further evidence for the hidden spiritual agenda operating at the time of the nation's founding were the many intriguing events documented at the time of the founding of the United States.

One concerns a mysterious gentleman who participated in the design of the flag.

He was a boarder at the home of a friend of one of the committee members assigned the task of designing the flag. This friend's home was chosen as the meeting place for the flag committee, a circumstance curious in itself. During the meeting it was decided that the six men present did not constitute "an auspicious number" and so the hostess was included in the meeting to raise their number to seven. (The number seven, numerologically, represents wisdom, in particular spiritual wisdom, and faith in a higher plan.) The stranger, known only as the "Professor," made suggestions as to the flag's design, discussing at length the significance of each element, which was unanimously adopted by the committee. The Professor was not seen again after this meeting even though he had had such an important role in designing the new nation's symbol.

Declaration of Independence

An even more mysterious event occurred at the time of the signing of the Declaration of Independence.

A strange man, unknown to all others present, somehow entered unobserved the old State House in Philadelphia where the signers were gathered. This was a time of great trepidation for those present, as they knew that the penalty that would be imposed by the Crown if they were caught was sure to be swift and merciless. The debate became heated as members argued the pros and cons of the instrument that would sever their ties to England. Suddenly, the stranger, as if possessed by some great power, bellowed out with a voice that resonated through the hall. He spoke eloquently and with great conviction, saying, in part:

"Sign that parchment! Sign, if the next moment the gibbet's rope is about your neck! Sign, if the next minute this hall rings with the clash of falling axes! Sign, by all your hopes in life or death, as men, as husbands, as fathers, brothers, sign your names to the parchment, or be accursed forever! Sign, and not only for yourselves, but for all ages, for that apartment will be the textbook of freedom, the bible of the rights of man forever. . .God has given America to be free!"

He collapsed into a chair as the glamour left him and the mood in the room changed from discord to harmonious enthusiasm for the task the Founders had come to perform. As the signers crowded around the document that would declare their freedom from tyrannical rule the mysterious stranger departed, unseen, even though the doors were locked and guarded.

Birthdate of a Nation

The date that was chosen for the birthdate of this nation was arrived at only through careful consideration. When we decode the July 4, 1776, date numerologically, we arrive at a striking result:

July 4—the 7th month + the 4th day, or 7.4. This 7.4 is an expression of the Messiah vibration:

$$M \quad E \quad S \quad S \quad I \quad A \quad H$$
$$13 + 19 + 19 + 8 \;\; = 59 \;\; (Consonants)$$
$$5 + 9 + 1 = 15 \;\; (Vowels)$$

$$59 + 15 = 74 \text{ (Numerical numbers for Messiah)}$$

One thing to note in the example above is that, in planetary numerology, we use double and triple digit numbers as well as the single digits that most numerologists use. For example, the letter M is the 13th letter of the alphabet, so we use 13 instead of the single-digit 4. Also, we separate consonants and vowels as part of the interpretation process.

The year, 1776, also has a significance, in that the numbers may be interpreted to mean "world". As such, July 4th, 1776, resonates with the phrase "World Messiah."

The Founding Fathers selected the only day of the year that could bring Messianic proportions to the new nation's birthdate. They knew the time had come for the energy of the Messiah to be introduced into governmental structure.

As long as the independence and freedom of the individual was of paramount importance in the language of the Declaration of Independence, this Messianic purpose would be transferred to the governance of the people on a symbolic and subconscious level.

Even though this energy was introduced on a symbolic level, its power was firmly grounded in the July 4, 1776 birthdate, ensuring the fulfillment of the higher purpose. This birthdate was the first time in history that the Messianic power of altruism, to be manifested in the form of the Light of the World, was grounded at the governmental level. The Founders' vision was extraordinary for their time in history.

Great Seal of the United States

The Great Seal of the United States is another example of the secret societies' influence on the symbolism that was chosen to represent the essence of the new nation. After two committees tried and failed to approve the design of the United States' Great Seal, a third committee approved the emblems designed by Charles Thomson and William Barton on June 20, 1782. The front of the seal is an eagle (or phoenix) and a shield. The reverse is a pyramid without a capstone over which the all-seeing eye is placed.

The reverse side of the shield went un-recut, even though the front side was recut several times, until Henry A. Wallace, the former Vice-President and Secretary of Agriculture, submitted a proposal to then-president Franklin D. Roosevelt to have the entire front and reverse sides recut in 1934.

Wallace enticed the President by interpreting the seal's motto Novus Ordo Seclorum (New Order of the Ages) to mean "The New Deal of the Ages." In any event, the fact that both men were Masons most certainly played a part in their interest in having the seal recut. They would have recognized the Masonic symbolism in the pyramid/all-seeing eye image on the reverse, which would explain why

Roosevelt decided, in 1935, to have it placed on the one-dollar bill.

Bald Eagle

The American bald eagle, who lives nobly and majestically on the higher cliffs, is firmly entrenched on the Great Seal, a symbol of U.S. lofty ideals. His breast is protected by a shield, as are U.S. individual rights protected by Congress.

The eagle's right claw clutches an olive branch, and in the left, thirteen arrows—signifying this government has the power of peace or war. However, the eagle's head is turned toward the olive branch of peace.

His beak holds a ribbon which blazes the motto, "E Pluribus Unum," meaning, "Out of many, one."

Above the eagle's head is a burst of thirteen stars signifying that the nation lifts the spiritual above the material.

US Dollar

On the back of the U.S. one dollar bill, in the left-hand corner, is the reverse of the Seal with an Egyptian pyramid, representing solid strength and direction. The pyramid has a raised cap, depicting the concept that the United States will always grow, building on truth.

Above the pyramid is the All-Seeing Eye of God—a symbol as ancient as time, directly from the Hierarchy teachings. It is surrounded by a triangle. The words above, "Annuit Coeptis," mean "God has favored our under-takings."

Below the pyramid are the words, "Novus Ordo Seclorum," meaning, "The New Order of the Ages." This truth is especially pertinent as the New Order comes into being.

The priceless heritage that came out of Egypt and other ancient lands has given America its present destiny. This destiny is in the memory pattern of the citizens of the United States and unity souls are beginning to recall their missions. They are arising to the unity responsibilities their heritage demands. Hierarchy could not have been more explicit as they overlighted the ordained Founding Fathers of this new country in 1776.

Symbol of the Sun

The symbol of the sun—shining as a focal point of our attention—is a constant reminder of the universality of light, love, wisdom, and power. The sun in the life of the solar system is the symbol that has brought illumination to the great initiates of the ancient wisdom schools. The sun has been the symbol of many spiritual groups of the past.

As Islam is concerned in the acceptance of the sun as the reflection light of the moon, the moon is the symbol of their faith, but still they referred to the same light and again in Christendom as the "Light of the World."

At least, these symbols give us food for thought. "Behold I am the Light of the world"—the same light, the same wisdom, the same plan—putting it in our own words, and working toward its manifestation, each in our own way. Now it is the responsibility of each of us to express the Light of the World for the benefit of all creation.

The Double-Headed Eagle—The Supreme Symbol

Here is depicted the Supreme Hierophant, Master of the double Holy Empire of the superior and the inferior universes. The ancient emblem of equilibrium consisted of an androgynous body surmounted by two heads, one male and the other female, wearing a single imperial crown.

That being alone is perfect in which all opposites are reconciled, and this state of perfection is appropriately typified by the two heads of equal dignity. Hence the double-headed eagle is reserved as the emblem of completion, for it signifies the Philosopher's Stone, the ultimate soul condition, and that absolute and transcendent perfection which arises only from the fullest unfoldment of the latent potentialities within the individual.

Philosophically, the thirty-third degree of the Ancient and Accepted Scottish Rite represents the innermost sanctuary of Masonic mysticism. If the double-headed eagle—the symbol of that sublime degree—were endowed with the power of speech, it would say:

"Only he may wear me in whom there is no guile: in whom all passion has been transmuted into compassion, all natural ignorance into divine wisdom, all selfishness into selflessness; for I am an ancient and a sacred emblem of all greatness, all perfection, and all truth.

"I represent a spiritual condition, a mental attitude, a physical state attained only by the elect of Earth. I am the symbol of the illumined and transfigured soul which has been born again and has approached the throne of Divinity. I am the symbol of the gatekeeper, for with one face I behold the radiant countenance of my Creator and with the other the expanse of the universe which He has fashioned.

"Upon my strong pinions of intuition and reason men have ascended to a position betwixt heaven and earth. He in whom I spread my wings is more than a man yet less than a god; therefore he is a god-man. I clutch between my talons the flaming cherubic sword, the flaming spirit-fire with which the miracle of my existence was wrought.

"I am the symbol of the Initiator who, through the ages, carries Ganymedes into the presence of the gods upon his back."

Hebrew History

Hebrew history is steeped in demonstrations of psychic phenomena. Judaism is a mystical religion.

Adam walked with God.   Abel heard the Lord's whisper.   Noah built an ark with plans received clairvoyantly. Abraham was guided by voices and visions. A voice came to Samuel. And there were over two hundred allusions to angels in the Old Testament.   Nearly one thousand references to psychic events.

Religion's distinctive feature is that it is deeply involved in and with the intuitional. Christianity cannot be separated from its beliefs in psychical events.   Paul's encounter on the road to Damascus, or a modern demonstration of glossolalia (speaking in a language previously unknown to the speaker) give proof that the roots of Christianity are deep in intuition.

Symbology is also found in the pyramid. The ancient Egyptian symbology contends the pyramid itself is the prophecy of the ultimate fulfillment of the last dispensation of the Christian era.   Beyond this last dispensation, prophecy no longer exists.

When you're at the Great Pyramid—and I've been there only 30 times—we have some private time, and basically, you are a pyramid, symbolically.

The capstone is the top of your head. This symbolizes the connection you have with the Divine.

Here's the king's chamber, your forehead, which is the superconscious mind. When we go there, we need to plant some seeds, embracing all the flags and nations of the planet. This is very sacred—all the flags and religions on Earth.

Here is the heart of the pyramid—near your heart—little places you have to crawl into. It's a symbol of the feminine energy, and the reason we have to crawl into it is because it is so difficult to be a woman. I have so much respect for women. Multi-faceted, multi-dimensional, giving, serving—it's unbelievable, and we get into that. When we get into the Queen's Chamber, we just pay tribute to all the mothers on planet Earth. We send it out to everyone—to thank them for being the mothers of this world.

Next we go up the grand gallery to the great pyramid. It's real straight up—there's no detours. So many times in life we take detours—we make mistakes.

Easter

On a personal level, Easter is a symbol of rebirth, positive change, and rededication to higher principles and ideals. Each Easter, we reevaluate our lives to determine what changes we can make within ourselves on physical, mental, and emotional levels.

With each goal of personal transformation, a plan must be made and implemented into a habit pattern for daily living. Time is a great ally when we are creating a brand-new habit pattern. Each day, we set aside specific time periods to meditate and exercise. The time on the clock indicates a reminder of what we promised ourselves we would do each day "without exception."

The two words "without exception" are the key to successful rebirth and resurrection into new positive lifestyles. The major habit shift becomes permanent when we continue to pick ourselves up, dust ourselves off, and start all over again. When our positive habit pattern moves into the same old past detour of "I didn't have time today to meditate and exercise because something else came up," then that same old habit pattern emerges. We just simply start all over again the next day.

If we continue to persevere to meditate and exercise the same time each day, a permanent Easter resurrection will manifest in our life as a daily commitment to excellence.

The Higher Chakras

The Sphinx is the place on the Nile where the initiates went up all the chakras. There was a priest or priestess waiting to determine if they'd earned the right to enter the great pyramid.

That last letter of the Sphinx—the X symbolizes ascension into higher consciousness.

A quick overview/analogy of the 8 – 13th chakras. That's where you are right now.

8th chakra – (Mind, Earth) Organization on all levels—money, time management, self-mastery, will. A personal and planetary and universal chakra—as above, so below. Look at the figure 8. The upper oval is the world, the lower is the Earth. The world is the mind of the Earth, and now we are in a position of becoming a Light of the World. That's your responsibility. Be the Sun. From the position of the higher oval of the 8, praying for the Earth. That symbolizes that infinity.

9th chakra represents altruism, selflessness, and compassion. Realizing that it's about everyone except us.

10th Chakra – Elimination of negative earth desires

11th Chakra – Existence on a high plane of intellect and spirituality

12th Chakra – Balance of feminine heart ad will of the mind

13th Chakra – Communication on multi levels of creation—Arthur/Jesus Mastery—how to handle difficult people in our lives

Snow White and the Seven Dwarfs

The allegory of Snow White and the Seven Dwarfs interestingly relates to our personal Easter story. Snow White is our soul that incarnates into this imperfect physical third dimension with our personal seven dwarfs symbolizing the lessons of our seven chakras.

We are in the third dimension to master each of our seven dwarf chakra challenges that we will learn by mastering our seven lower desires. Each of us are working on different chakras to master in a given lifetime. "One man's meat is another man's poison." We should never judge another in their quest for their personal chakra mastery that we have already conquered. We may be facing their particular chakra test in another lifetime.

"The Judas Betrayal" would be one of our chakras betraying our mental attempt to master that particular chakra's lower desire. Our Easter ascension takes place when we eventually conquer our own Judas Iscariot desires. We have to continue to forgive our dwarf desire for failing so many times before, and then ultimately move into a life of altruistic service—helping others to conquer that desire we have personally conquered.

The significance of Judas in Jesus' great life is the story of the past Judases in our life being ultimately forgiven and to stop looking back "to review our autopsies." We eventually learn to forgive the Judas Edwards in our life when they appear as important people in our lives such as our boss, ex-spouse, friends who have betrayed us. They are mirrors in this life because we were just like them in our previous lives. We ultimately succeed in spite of the past influence of our past Judas figures because we finally realize the important of not looking back and saying, "Why did I attract them into my life in the first place?"

The realization of that pain of experiencing and enduring the Judas figures bring us literally into our heart and the center of the cross Jesus carried to Calvary (his heart) and the center of the cross in our physical body (our heart), we carry it for a lifetime and it brings us to active lives of compassion, self-sacrifice, and unconditional love. As these personal goals are embraced, we understand the fantastic symbology of the magnificent Easter season.

Three Kings Appear

At Jesus' birth, three kings appeared to him as well as to each of us at our birth.

The first king (Will) symbolizes the first three major challenges each person must face on the earth plane— money, sex, and power. The second king (Commitment) reminds us that the practical ways to accomplish our personal objectives are diet, meditation, and exercise. The third king (Success) reminds us that humility, love, and service are the ultimate goals to achieve in this life when we love ourselves enough to master the illusory laws of money, sex, and power by following and practicing the daily habits of diet, meditation, and exercise.

Coptic Secret Texts

Six thousand years ago, Hermes the Great—a Master Teacher—lived and taught in Egypt. After him came Buddha, Moses, and finally, Jesus the Christ. All messengers carried the same simple message.

For many years, Moses gave the doctrine of truth to the Israelites, and when the time approached for him to leave his physical body, he called together a chosen few to whom he entrusted the guardianship of the truth. To these he gave certain secret knowledge that was to be preserved and passed on to other specially selected ones, the secret order known as the Essenes.

Their duty was to preserve the teachings given to them by Moses and await the coming of Jesus the Christ, whose birth he prophesied would be heralded by a star.

The secret order of the Essenes, of which the Holy Family were members, had guarded the Word for eons of time.

The Essenes' ancient heritage was to utilize symbols so the Word would remain hidden. By word of mouth and secret writings, the law was passed on, carried forth from generation to generation, through careful teaching for the undiluted message.

The mass of humankind has received only symbolic smatterings of the Word, dissipating and fracturing it to satisfy their own special desires and limited vision.

The Word, out of necessity, has remained hidden, century upon century.

Christian Bible Altered

Though many great truths found their way into the Holy Bible, many misconceptions also developed.

This Bible is composed of 39 books or manuscripts comprising the Old Testament, and 27 in the New Testament, all of which were written over a period of time from 2,000 B. C. to 150 A. D.

Much of the Bible cannot be interpreted literally but is rather an inspirational, historical, philosophical, and prophetic book. The Bible is a guide to life on the three-fold nature of man—spiritual, mental, and physical.

The New Testament introduces a New Order, based on the appearance and teaching of a new Master. Much of the teaching is mystical—the unfolding of the descent of the Spirit to the physical Jesus. The entire Biblical work has a symbolic overtone.

In the Bible we read, "I will build me a temple in Egypt." The prophecy is dual in nature. Coptic Masters took this statement to mean Jesus' body being the Temple in Egypt since he was taken as a babe, then later returned after age 12 to receive more intensified training. He was put in contact with the Coptic Order, known as the Essaioi, which embraced the so-called Christian philosophy after Jesus' later Egyptian training.

The Bible, particularly the New Testament containing the words of Jesus, has been revised many times, with most of the revisions done to suit the translators.

We seem to be in the same situation today spiritually as were the Jews when Jesus came to deliver an urgent message of inspiration and truth to the spiritually hungry people of Israel.

Despite their hunger, Jesus' simple words were rejected because their meaning did not fit the traditionalized religion of Moses. People of Israel had molded their religion to fit themselves instead of yielding to the truth of His message.

It was during the time of the Inquisition that many of Jesus' teachings were deleted from the sacred writings, especially teachings on reincarnation (Law of Rebirth) and karma (Law of Cause and Effect) that was an integral part of the knowledge of Jesus' day.

This removal of these two original books from the Bible was a deliberate desecration of the teachings of the Hierarchy by leaders who wanted to keep the populace under their control. They perpetrated false teachings, creating fear and superstition among the unlearned, and separated East from West with a deep chasm of misunderstanding.

It was, in certain areas of the planet, a time of darkness for humanity. It must not happen again. Hierarchy must show humanity that they can lay aside their dogma and look at their fellow beings with tolerance and forgiveness.

Essenes Records Hidden

Since the Essenes were a secret order, their records have been hidden. Information they wanted to make public is found in the writings of Philo and Josephus—two Jewish philosophers who wrote in Greek.

Philo wrote, "Palestine and Syria, too, which are inhabited by no slight portion of the numerous population of the Jews, are not barren of virtue. There are some among them called Essaioi—in number more than four thousand— from an incorrect derivation from the Greek homonym 'Hosiotes,' meaning Holiness, because they are above all other worshippers of God."

Josephus gives information on the initiation of membership into the Essenes. Initiation was most demanding to be certain The Word would be safeguarded until it could be passed on in pure form. The demands made upon disciples were the most stringent training a person could endure.

Select in membership, demanding absolute obedience in bringing forth the Word as given by God, unwavering, persevering everywhere on the earth plane, these pure and dedicated souls have understood and loved the light so deeply that they have stood unmoving and dedicated against greed and selfishness, and did not permit the diluting of the Word.

The mantle of authority was revered by those who took the vows, for it was given in complete love and devotion. Only those who had spiritual eyes to see, and ears to hear, and unyielding will could quality for these sacred tasks.

Mary, the mother of Jesus, was one of the highest initiates of the women to be admitted to the Essene order. Mary's divine nature gave to the order a feminine essence that enriched this closcly knit group.

The Essenes cherished and guarded the pure philosophy of Moses through a changing and tempestuous world until the birth of Jesus the Christ.

Having kept such control, the Word has remained pure, as the fickleness of humankind intermittently warmed or cooled to the messages of the prophets.

Such precious secrets were kept from those with self-serving motivations.

Essene Community

Their community was solid in common purpose, and always benevolent.

They did not lay up treasures of gold and silver, nor acquire large parcels of land. Humble, living simply by world measures, they were materially poor, but they considered themselves rich, for they firmly believed completely that God was their source of provision for everything they needed.

They neither bought nor sold anything among themselves, generously sharing their material possessions with one another, as they believed they were stewards of God's bounty. The Essenes had the freedom to help and show mercy to the needy.

They demonstrated their love of God through their consistent and unalterable holiness, their complete honesty in their dealings with all men and women. They understood the importance of keeping the soul, mind, and body healthy, balanced, and pure as possible.

The Essenes were strong-willed and one-minded in their sacred responsibilities. They were persecuted by members of their own faith, ridiculed and misunderstood, but their divine purpose was so deeply ingrained, they could not violate their shared trust.

The ruler Herod had great respect for the Essenes, yet he often forgot his piety in order to bring honor and power to himself.

When the Romans invaded their homes, the Essenes were among the most persecuted. They were tortured, put upon the rack, burned upon pyres of fire, subjected to all instruments of torture, yet they did not blaspheme their lawgivers. Enduring through their torments and never mocking their tormentors, they went gloriously to their deaths, surrendering their physical bodies, knowing they were eternal.

They believed that the soul was immortal, so when released by death, they would rejoice in the soul's physical departure and freedom from servitude.

The Holy Family fled to Egypt for safety, and Jesus was placed under the care of High Egyptian Masters. It was the Essenes who cared for the Christ Child in Egypt until Herod's death.   Thus, they provided a body for the incarnation of the Christ just as their forefathers—the Great White Brotherhood—had provided a body for the incarnation of the Messiah in the body of Moses. Jesus was born of Essene parentage.

The Essenes fulfilled their responsibilities as designated by the Hierarchy in guarding the truth of the Word.

The White Brotherhood fulfilled their sacred responsibilities by preserving the truth in its pure form. They provided a protective group for nurturing the incarnation of the Messiah through Moses.

Moses' prophecy was manifested in the coming of the New Messiah, the incarnation of the Christ through the man Jesus, whose Israelite name was Issa, given to Jesus during an initiation in Egypt at the age of 12.

The Essenes had seers and prophets who foretold future events.   They very seldom failed in their predictions, for they were schooled from youth in the sacred scriptures and the hidden secrets of the prophets.

Before Jesus made his transition, He declared that the organization that would continue teaching the Word as given by the White Brotherhood should be called "Coptic." The existence of this secret organization carrying "The Word" has never been revealed during the time of its existence, but history always records it for later revelation.

Christian Coptic Order

The Christian Coptic Order originated in a temple in Cairo, Egypt, where Jesus had been taken by His parents on their flight from Bethlehem.

126

Jesus founded the Christian Coptic Order for the purpose of preserving His teachings, pure and unadulterated, until the next Christ Consciousness should again manifest itself in human form.

The Coptic Secret Order was especially created for the safekeeping of the original Christian teachings, founded by St. Mark in 70 A. D.

Thirty-seven years after the crucifixion of Jesus the Christ, St. Mark was appointed as first Christian Patriarch.

The Holy Family remained in this sanctuary until after Herod died. The sanctuary then became a shrine, being used as a place of worship as early as 217 A.D. However, the first Christian Coptic church was not built until 1117 in Cairo.

The first people in Egypt to become Christians were the Pharaohs, who embraced Christianity in 217 A.D., at which time the name Coptic was adopted.

The Coptic Church of Egypt, the Coptic Church of Ethiopia, the Greek Orthodox Coptic Religion and the Coptic Fellowship of America are branches of the same Christian tree.

The Coptic Order is now fulfilling their role as did the Essenes. They possess truths which can be of great benefit to many, but these truths can be given only to individuals who reach the state of spiritual development necessary to their proper reception.

Humanity is now enlightened enough that previously secret teachings can be disclosed and have been revealed, in fact, by many enlightened beings representing unity-motivated groups through the Earth.

During this age in history, much information is being brought forth through souls of many religions who have attuned themselves to higher dimensions where the Akashic records are anchored.

The time is almost upon us when the Word shall be given.

Section 5:
The Light of the World

NOW is the Time

At the start of each millennium, a time period of nine years represents a time bridge of energy from one millennium to another. During this important time period, prototypes from the previous millennium step forth to show humanity the lessons we have to learn before the next spiritual age begins. Major leaders in commerce, religion, and politics step up, and show us by their actions and deeds and demonstrate by their dramatic personal examples of the best things to achieve and what to avoid for the next 1,000 years.

January 1, 2000, was the first day of the new millennium. The energies of the Sun and Archangel Michael were present on that day. The planetary energy of the sun will positively impact the Earth for the next 1,000 years. Our individual responsibility is to project the energies of the inner and outer sun to all peoples and nations in prayer and positive action.

A major planetary shift started on January 1, 2008. Based on the ancient science of planetary numerology, according to many, this date represents the actual birth of the Aquarian Age. This date is a major shift into new planetary beginnings with no subconscious challenges, a very rare occurrence on the planetary level.

Around 1900, Alice Bailey, and the many books she wrote, discussed in depth the emergence of a new group of World Servers who would be living in the early 2000's to initiate the Aquarian Age through the power of positively motivated group prayer (fire). Jesus represents the opening of the planetary heart chakra (water). A new group of World Servers with their minds are the instruments of the Aquarian Age (air). As we visualize the level six chakra demonstrated by the Sphinx and Great Pyramid, the new group of World Servers' mission is simply fulfilled by individual and group prayers on the Aquarian Age birth date 1/1/2008. To accomplish this mission, World Servers through the Earth move mentally into a multi-world dimension. This is a world mission through the acceptance of certain simple principles embracing the future vision of humanity by understanding the concept of "the world as one family" in multi-diversities. We are praying for the positive and prosperous evolution of Earth's creation.

Christ and Buddha

As Buddha manifested Light, so the Christ is the principle of Love, also possessing the qualities of the Buddha Light. Christ is the personification of love and service, admonishing man to love one another. We are encouraged to share wisdom we have acquired. No exclusive order exists in the Kingdom of God. Universal energy is of love. What might appear to be punishment is simply the law of cause and effect a person brings upon oneself through freedom of choice. It is the law of nature working out to its own natural conclusion. The many Lights of the World will help bring light and love into manifestation.

While on Earth, Christ through Jesus taught that our Mother-Father God is a God of love, the human spirit is eternal, and that the physical body is only the temporary vehicle which eventually returns to disintegration. He taught that the Spirit, the love and light, is present in everyone, but best expressed through universal love and selfless service to humanity.

The Lights of the World are returning to Earth and welcome all men and women of all religions, philosophies,

and nationalities.   All individuals who are inspired by
Divine Spirit—no matter what church or denomination—are
children of God. The task of the Aquarian Age will be to
unify peoples and nations into a loving worldwide fellowship, serving humanity everywhere, under a unified world
philosophy of diversity. Every church that has personified
God as the loving God of all mankind has an inherent basis
of truth, but no church on the earth plane today possesses
total truth. Acceptance of men and women everywhere is a
divine prerequisite for the coming world peace and the
planetary Sister/Brotherhood the Lights of the World will
promote.

Christ Consciousness refers to conscious recognition of
the inner Lights of the World principle that exists in every
individual awaiting manifestation. If Light of the World
awareness is dormant, inevitably an incarnation will come
which will inspire the heart and mind of that individual on
the path home to perfect oneness with the Source.
Eventually, nothing can prevent the soul's homeward
journey.   The memory and longing will, in some
incarnation, bring the soul to the path of return, this pattern
imprinted at the time of individualization.

First Aspect – Willpower

The first aspect of the universal return corresponds to
the willpower ray, and deals with the return of universality
in the form of individual consciousness. The universal
return in this manner will be through the activation of the
willpower ray, to bring forth universal consciousness on an
individual level.

It will be through the activation of this aspect of the
universal return which will bring about the great cleansing
for humanity and for the planet. This cleaning can be a very

beautiful, gentle, and benevolent experience if activated on an individual basis and carried out from the individual unto the cleansing of the entire world through individual action.

Second Aspect – Group Effort

The second aspect of the return of the Light of the World will be through group effort of those who are conscious of the Light of the World energy. This corresponds to the Suns of the Trinity.

It will be through group effort of Christ Conscious individuals that Love and Wisdom will manifest on the Earth through the channel of the Suns of God who shall walk on the Earth and share the knowledge and Love of God. Through the expression of World Light unto humanity in this way, humankind will again be presented the opportunity to become World Light Conscious and manifest the Light of God from within.

By the activation of the Love and Wisdom through group effort, the impact of the cleansing force can be eased and utilized more as a constructive energy for humanity rather than a destructive energy. All religions and philosophies should unite as Light Conscious individuals to form a network of Light over the face of the Earth and ease the Karmic debts of the world as well as raise the Light Consciousness in humanity. "Where two or more are gathered together in my name, there also I AM," is factual on many levels in the manifestation of the Second Aspect of the World Light.

The most powerful and real manifestation being the return through the I AM that I AM. It will be through the channeling of light—the Light from within—and the linking of the hearts and Minds of those Light Conscious individuals, that Universal Love may manifest fully on the Earth.

The second phase is moving rapidly in developing peace upon the Earth. The coming of the World Light within has been well defined. Dedicated souls are experiencing this birth throughout the Earth in every land. There is not a city, a hamlet, or a countryside where the World Light has not come into the hearts of humankind. This has brought great light upon the Earth, dissipating much darkness.

The Third Aspect – Light of the World

The third aspect of the Light of the World return will come after the expression of the first two aspects have been felt and enacted upon the Earth. This relates to the Holy Spirit of the Trinity.

As Buddha manifested the Will, the Father, and Christ Master Jesus, manifested love and wisdom, so shall the Lights of the World manifest the active intelligence, the Holy Spirit. It will be through the expression of the Light of the World that readied men and women shall again be shown the true potential of the Spirit and the way to obtain liberation.

Hierarchy to Raise Humanity

One of the principal functions of the Hierarchy is to raise humanity to higher spiritual levels. Throughout the ages, a small number of Great Ones has always manifested on the earth plane to work physically with their aspiring brothers and sisters. These Great Masters have mingled with humanity unrecognized, rendering service wherever they were, living examples of unconditional love.

The Great Council at Shamballa determined to introduce the Spiritual Kingdom to the physical levels by letting their members manifest on the earth plane in greater numbers, functioning in closer and more conscious contact with humanity.

Many spiritual servants are reincarnating now at this time of history, but before the Masters can more openly work in full recognition, there must come a greater change. Though much progress has been made, we must advance much more rapidly if we are to receive the maximum benefit of the refined higher wisdom of the Ascended masters.

Ancient Wisdom Restored

The New Age will come gradually, not all at once, just like Jesus the Christ's Dispensation did not take root immediately. Jesus' Disciples worked hard for many, many years and the same will be true concerning the Aquarian Age. We are now witnessing the day of the signs and wonders that precede the opening of the New Dispensation.

The manifestation of Hierarchy on the Earth will be a gradual process, but eventually the ancient wisdom will be restored here to be promoted through education as the new world religion of unity through diversity develops. The Masters' influence is already being felt, particularly in communities that have assumed the responsibility of selfless service. Only a continuing down- pouring of love from the upper spiritual realms will bring about accelerated change. This streaming of light and love is being observed in many areas such as goodwill, compassion, and selfless service.

The momentum of spiritual interest is changing worldwide, therefore the Lights of the World will also have many active members from different parts of the world.

The Lights of the World have already been activated into many physical bodies. One of the primary reasons for this paradigm shift is that now enough souls on Earth have become Universal Conscious. During the Earth's 11th hour of evolution, it is necessary to plant the Universal Light seed in all religions and philosophies now ready for the change. If humble hearts are ready, the Universal Light seed will be reborn again and again in many individuals, religions, and eventually, nations. If put on a worldwide level, the Lights of the World are waiting of the timing to be right for the Heart of the Earth to be humble enough to accept Universal teachings, merging all nations and denominations into ONE.

Sons & Daughters of God

Sons and daughters of God have filled their beings with light, bringing forth universal love energy. They are assuming responsibility for manifesting the World Light in their homes, their work, and in their recreation. Wherever they go, whatever they say and do, they have the inner light that directs them in their responsibility to live truth and love. Joy shines upon their countenance and in their activities. They move to the music of the spheres, dancing in the light and in the shadows, flowing with this new-found awakening. This inner and outer projection of love has, indeed, dissipated much of the destructive energy that has formed in and around the Earth. This is bringing about the second phase of the World Light return.

As individuals have brought forth the light within themselves, and developed their potential, maturity, and love, they have gathered to share their enlightenment. Sons and daughters of God have gathered together in common fellowship, sitting in silence to hear the voice of God as they call upon the vibrations of the universe to pour forth its cleansing fire.   As light energy gathers within groups everywhere, more light has increased.   These explosions are happening all over Earth, in a kaleidoscope of fabric rainbows.

Through word and song, the energy has grown, the light is coming forth into loving and responsible groups at a tremendous rate.   The Hierarchy has been able to use this anchored light, and has scattered much negative energy that would have caused even greater chaos upon the plane of matter.   The foretold vortexes of negative energy created by wrong thinking through the space of time has been dispensed by love expressed through individuals and groups that have sustained the light, dissipating the darkness.

All Energy is God

This unified strength connects with the energy flowing from our sun, which is a reflection of the Central Sun, which is God.   Humanity intuitively recognizes that all energy is God, and God is light and sound.

Light is manifesting in a trillion different energy patterns and vibratory rates that bring forms of intricate variety.   All that is is vibrating at its own individual rate, giving it special shape and size.   Everything that is has life.

Knowing this, each individual bows his or her head in awe and humility, acknowledging the light within and without.   This is the meaning of the Second World Birth in the form of groups working together in harmony and cooperation.

Unity in diversity is the foundation of heightened vision, not the bringing of groups together for purposes of conformity.

Earth's 11th Hour

We presently live at a critical turning point in Earth's history. People in every nation on the planet have felt the pull toward a spiritual unification of the human family and have responded to the call from Spirit by establishing groups devoted to the promotion of planetary peace.

Because of humanity's individualized manifestation, brought forth eons ago, many have wandered far from the source, but are now lonely for fellowship with Father-Mother God. This is the basic cause of the restlessness of the creation called human, who dwells upon this planet and throughout the universe in individualized form.

The family of humanity upon the earth plane has been fluctuating in darkness and light for endless time as measured by Earth calculation. Now by remembering their beginning as being part of the source, they have cried out to their Creator, asking for light upon their countenance and in their hearts. The Source, the Father-Mother God, has heard the cry of the world's children, and has responded.

Not since humanity became entrapped in the physical kingdom of earth plane has the cry for salvation been so loud and anguished. The forces of light manifesting as an extension of the Godhead have been directed to intervene. It has been determined that the civilization of humankind shall be permitted to return to universality. This earth plane shall not perish, but it shall, in the next short span of time, undergo a thorough cleansing and purification.

During the Earth's 11th hour of evolution, it is necessary to plant the Light of the World Light seed in all religions and for philosophies to be ready to accept their role as the Light of the World. If our humble heart is ready, this light seed will be born within us.

The 11th hour is the last hour, the purest hours of human existence.

The 11th hour usually pertains to a great Master or a Messiah. Masters have no personal designs—only that of spiritual purposes, no other motivations. That is why the dominant presence of the number 11—the 11th hour, 11th day of the 11th month.

The 12th hour is the descendent. We reach up again, the soul ascends at the 12th hour. At the gate at the 12th hour—the passage—we progress across the lake to the boat of Khufu and enter into the spiritual world.

It was the Great Christ who said, "Now is the appointed time," because in Divine Consciousness, it is always Now. And in the sense of Nowness you can achieve the sense of Oneness, oneness with Christ, oneness with Hierarchy, oneness with the Great Light, and become the Light of the World.

Light of the World as Symbol of Freedom

The spiritual manifestation of the Light of the World—which is the symbol of freedom and liberation of the soul—is permeating the Earth with urgency.

World light energy is a magnetic force drawing people together in fellowship. When humanity becomes willingly lighted with the universal spirit, and allows its manifestation in thoughts and actions—plus a concerted effort toward spiritual unity—universal light and love can occur.

The great universal appearance is imminent! The signs and wonders are upon us. Those who have eyes to see and ears to hear have seen and heard. They are aware that the first phase of the universal return must be in the hearts of those who are ready to recognize their beginning. The spirit of God shall become one with them and the flesh will be made pure by the Holy Spirit that shall come upon them like the flowing river of golden fire.

The Angels and Archangels have declared the glory of the coming of universality into the hearts of humanity. Only as the higher consciousness comes into the total being of humankind will the actual physical appearance of the new reality be made! This has been God's promise from the beginning of time when humans manifested upon the Earth in physical form.

Creating a Better World

In case you hadn't noticed, December 21, 2012 passed without a major cataclysmic incident.

Edgar Cayce and Michael Nostradamus appeared on the world scene at a most important time in planetary history. When these two giants appeared, humanity had reached the 11th hour in the cosmic clock of planetary time (one hour remained). If the inner thought patterns and the outer focus of humanity did not change to positivity, world peace, and sharing, then many of their prophecies may have come to pass.

The prophetic timeline in the Great Pyramid has ended, and humanity stands at the 12:00 hour when its image casts no shadow. In other words, the future now rests in the hands of a collective humanity to make mature decisions regarding Earth changes for the benefit of the world as a whole, not only in the best interest of any one individual, country, or religion.

When discussing Earth changes and prophecies regarding the future, written and oral testament has always been the same—a negative prophecy fulfilled is a prophecy failed. Until any Earth event actually happens, it can always be changed.   Future Earth changes can be modified by positive thought and prayer.

The common person has a definite impact on the trend of the world events. The responsibility of creating a better world rests in the hands of those individuals who accept the idea that thoughts are really things of power and change.

Before we go any further, we have to explain the difference between the world and the Earth. The world is a cumulative effect of the ideas, emotions, goals, and ambitions of the eight billion individuals residing (collective computer of world thought) and then reflects like a mirror back into the world of matter. The Earth is the body, the world is the mind.

In other words, what we think individually (the world) has a definite impact on what happens in the body (the Earth). By opening ourselves up to the ultimate possibility of projecting the goals of world peace, world healing, and work sharing every day we assist the many levels of consciousness on the other side in creating a better world for Earth inhabitants.

Return of the Light

One of the signs that more light is coming will be that key responsibilities in local, state, and national governments will be assumed by people who are overlighted by the universal principle. Many of these men and women will be highly evolved spiritually. Many of these world servers are becoming aware that they are being used by Hierarchy to help in the transition from the Old Age into the New Aquarian Consciousness.

The Light of the World is presently returning by the collective energy that has built a wall of beauty and light around the Earth. If one could be high enough above the

Earth, the Earth aura would look like a beautiful light circling the Earth.

Made of vibrations of all thoughts, ideas, emotions, goals, and objectives of individuals and collectively of nations, this circle of dense energy is enlightened by humankind's elevated thoughts of world peace and goodwill, invoking the light, converting and transmuting darkness into more light essence.

The New Age will bring a new civilization of goodwill, peace, and better human relations, resulting in one humanity, diversified world religions, one world order.

To bring this about, most of the emphasis upon the old order has to be altered—much of it has already been changed. The urgency in men and women everywhere to desire and declare openly their need for freedom is partly because the light is overlighting the Earth, insisting upon, most of all, a freedom of choice to take the steps necessary to become a Light of the World.

God responds, the individual responds, and more energy is focused. It is a flow of spiraling need and response that increases inner communication between people and their Source.

The coming of the Lights of the World is at hand to give guidance as to how the planetary plan shall be carried out. This manifestation is now upon us.

Will the human family respond in their hearts to the concept of planetary unification?

Know the forces of light are waiting to flood the Earth with their glory, lighting the path of humankind as they journey home.

After these times of transition are completed, glorious liberties await the Earth. First must come religious freedom. We must be set free of all preaching of hell, fire, and damnation that has been taught to the mass consciousness.

We must yield to the highest truth, the universal principle within us.

The fermenting of the Word is rising throughout the bread of mankind, as the sun of the new day brings the Solar Logos closer to the time clock of the Earth's peoples. It shall soon be the time of the breaking of the bread in a common feast of light and love.

Utopia on Earth

Ryoho Okawa, the Buddhist Master, writes in *The Laws of the Sun*:

"If tens of thousands, or millions, of people all had a desire to create a Land of Buddha or Utopia on Earth, and if they all focused their will on the task, a beam of light would spring out of the Earth and this light would filter into the minds of others until the whole world became a happier place.

"World Goodwill, an organization that was founded to assist in "establishing right human relations," speaks of the New Group of World Servers, or in our terms, the Light of the World. These World Servers are described as:

"[People who are] serving humanity, and are, through the power of their response to the spiritual opportunity, tide and note, emerging out of every class, group, church, party, race and nation and are therefor truly representative. They speak all languages; they embrace all religions, all sciences and all philosophies. . .[they] are so inclusive in their outlook and so wide in their interpretation of truth they are the hand of God in all happenings. . .

"These are the people who will change our world. We are seeing the influence of these visionaries as we search for peaceful solutions to our global problems. And their work is rooted in the ideal of unity."

In today's highly interdependent world, individuals and nations can no longer resolve many of their problems by themselves. We need one another. We must therefore develop a sense of universal responsibility. . . It is our collective and individual responsibility to protect and nurture the global family, to support its weaker members, and to reserve and tend to the environment in which we all live.

- His Holiness the Dalai Lama

Organizations Involved

There is much yet to be done. Humanity still has many lessons to learn, but they are rising to the challenge. They are asking for and accepting their spiritual homework. The signs and wonders of the New Age are abounding. As individuals and groups accept their responsibility, the light pours forth into energy, bringing about knowledge and wisdom to care for the neglected children of God.

The collective heart and intellect of humanity is now working to solve the problems of hunger and deprivation throughout the Earth. Individuals are beginning to feel responsible for their neighbors. Groups are beginning to be attuned to a sense of responsibility toward their brothers and sisters. They want no one to be hungry or cold.

As groups are receiving the bounty from their seeding and harvesting in material goods, they are sharing with their needy neighbors. Their sharing will bring peace upon the Earth, for where universal love reigns, wars and want cannot. This is the fulfillment of the law of love.

It is this phase of the master plan as designed by Hierarchy that the sons and daughters of God are now promoting.

Gathering Into Groups

The consciousness of the imminent arrival of the Group World Light has moved humanity's direction outward, giving them a different perspective of their world.

They have to seek for those souls who are also preparing for the World Light Way-showers. Their combined energies gather together in group form, conspiring to bring light and energy to their neighbors so they too can know the joy of the arrival.

Intuitively knowing from the beginning that humanity is one, they recognize inherent truth through many physical incarnations upon the earth plane—as well as on other planes and planets—but a veil has overshadowed their conscious minds, dimming their remembrance of their Source.

This veil has allowed them to see only faintly the truth that once flowed so strongly through their veins and sinews. This veil was formed to protect their fragile spirits, prompting self-development.

As individualized beings grow by lessons learned through trial and error, they move throughout the Earth at different levels of enlightenment. Each positive thought, each loving deed adds depth to the soul. Individuals use this Earth school of learning through many incarnations, according to their desires. Had there been no veil, then no testing would have occurred, with little soul expansion.

Gathering together into small groups greatly increases positive energy acquisition. Many groups have heard the call and have courageously gone out to sow the seeds of light, love, and service. God has promised the harvesting of the fruit, and it shall increase a thousandfold, even doubling and tripling that power as the sons and daughters of God bring forth the light.

The power of their energy is expanding and bringing light and joy wherever they move. As they go forward into the New Age, their kind shall increase. By the living example, and demonstration of universal love, they are touching the hearts of fellow beings everywhere, making their joy enticing to reluctant brothers and sisters who begin their own slow drum beat in response. The tempo increases.

This energy is reaping the harvest of love, balancing karma—personal and collective (law of cause and effect)—expanding health and wholeness to bodies and minds; all where darkness and despair had previously been harbored. The light diffuses and spreads, capturing the hearts and intellects of mankind. Thus the second phase of the World Light return is stirring throughout the Earth.

We should consider different groups who go under different names as radiant Sun Rays. All groups are a part of the group of world servers with the idea of working toward the Spiritual Unity of Nations—or by whatever name the ideal is called.

We should look upon the efforts of bygone teachers as stepping stones toward the fulfillment of the greatest need of all time—to unify humanity by God Power, Spiritual Power, so that even the nations will eventually come to a sense of change.

Esoteric Traditions

Down through the ages, the esoteric traditions of the Mystery Schools have been kept alive by individuals directed toward the evolution of mankind to achieving a higher spiritual ideal. These traditions were adopted by secret societies, whose membership boasted many high-ranking and learned members of the cultures of their time.

Manly P. Hall has concluded after studying ancient records of various cultures, that there has existed, over millennia, a group of enlightened souls which works toward the goal of world democracy. It is fair to say that these individuals often operate within the traditions of secret orders. Hall believes that a decision was made by these illumined minds, sometime "prior to the time of Plato," to create a "philosophic empire," based upon the democratic ideal, in the Western hemisphere, citing references to such a plan in Plato's writings on Atlantis.

One such New Age group that goes back into ancient times and follows the teachings of the Masters are the Rosicrucians. They are a community of Seekers who study and practice the metaphysical laws governing the universe. Their symbol is a cross in the center of the Mystical Rose.

Perhaps the most ancient of groups is the Masonic Order.

The Master Masons—the builders of temples and cities in ancient and modern times—had knowledge of the laws of the universe as given directly by the Masters of Hierarchy. Being master builders, they knew the laws of mathematics, triangles, and squares created the Pyramids and other magnificent temples in Egypt, Mexico, and other areas of the Earth, many yet to be discovered. They understood law, and practiced Truth as defined by law.

They banded together in the dawn of history to protect themselves from persecution. Persecutions lasted through the ages, but they have kept the original precepts of their order—their ritual—carrying them forward, most of them by word of mouth. Their ceremonies of initiation come from teachings far more ancient than the pyramids.

Their membership is spread worldwide. The feminine aspect of their teachings is expressed by the women's organization, the Eastern Star, for the Masons understood the positive and passive balance, that the feminine and masculine aspect of the universe must be maintained and promoted actively, for the feminine leadership role in Aquarius is absolutely necessary.

Founding Fathers

Organizations such as the Freemasons and Rosicrucians are prominent examples of secret societies established for the promotion of democratic principles and equality for all humanity, and both have had such astute persons as George Washington, Benjamin Franklin, Sir Francis Bacon and probably Thomas Jefferson in their ranks.

A thorough examination of the esoteric influences acting at the time of the founding of our country reveals the exquisite design underlying the development of the American nation.

Sir Francis Bacon was the architect of the English colonization of America, and undoubtedly saw it as the perfect environment in which to incubate the seeds of democracy. Bacon was a primary proponent of colonization of the New World, and exerted a great deal of influence on Queen Elizabeth I to do so. His prime motivation being to prevent Spain and the Catholic League from dominating the Western hemisphere.

He established Freemasonry and Rosicrucianism in the colonies before the middle of the 17th century and took great pains to indoctrinate the colonists with the ideals of religious tolerance, democratic government, and social equality.

In 1627, Bacon wrote The New Atlantis, a novel which was never published in total, but according to Hall, a second unpublished part exists and is well known among the secret societies of Europe. The book gives a blueprint of world democracy where each nation is equally represented, and all share in new discoveries in the arts and sciences, and great libraries hold all the world's knowledge. Interestingly, an illustration on the title page represents a great creature symbolizing Time leading a female figure out of a dark cave. Isn't that a fitting symbol for the emergence and empowerment of the feminine principle in the consciousness of our planet?

When the Founding Fathers convened to sculpt the foundation of our new nation, it was not without a great deal of consideration and deliberation. At least nine of the signers of the Declaration of Independence were Freemasons. Some historians claim as many as 50 of the Founding Fathers were Freemasons. While missing records make verification of this claim difficult if not impossible, records do exist that show unquestionably that George Washington, Benjamin Franklin, and probably Thomas Jefferson were Freemasons, and that Jefferson was most certainly a Rosicrucian, as evidenced by the discovery of a very old Rosicrucian code in his personal papers.

Freemasonry was in widespread practice in the 18th century, in both the New World and in Europe. Lafayette and Voltaire, both close associates of the Founders, were prominent Freemasons as were twelve of Washington's generals, who held membership in what were called "military lodges." All of this points to a grand esoteric design operating at the birth of the new republic, a design that had as its core the ideals of freedom of information and the elimination of political and religious tyranny.

The occult was an important element in the lives of the three aforementioned Founders. Benjamin Franklin was well known to have been proficient in astrology and alchemy, and his Poor Richard's Almanac was a popular publication that featured astrological information, which was of great interest to the colonists. Franklin also subscribed to the principle of reincarnation, the evidence for which is contained in his epitaph, which he wrote after a close brush with death due to an acute illness.

George Washington was no stranger to the occult either, and in fact, was the subject of two prophecies. One was a vision he had while stationed with his troops at Valley Forge in which an angel appeared to him and revealed America's future. The second was an Indian prophecy which foretold that Washington would be the founder and "chief" of a great nation of a diverse people.

And Thomas Jefferson, who was well versed in a variety of subjects, designed the University of Virginia, the structure of which, according to one researcher, contains the teaching of the Mystery Schools, leading one to conclude that he, too, had more than a passing interest in occult philosophy.

Birth of the USA

The forefathers of this land of America were sent by the Hierarchy of God to establish a pattern of rule that could eventually guide all nations in freeing its citizens and bring peace and spiritual unfoldment to the planet Earth.

The Bill of Rights and the Constitution were designed by men inspired by holy beings who saw to it that such concepts deemed important were hammered out in long, often wearying sessions, that became, on occasion, heated and inharmonious.

These were simple men in early days of the settling and organization of the new land, indentured servants of severe task masters, and slaves of exploiters in other lands. As they took on this personal universal consciousness in welding a new nation of freedom, they grew large in vision and began to sense the guidance of the Hierarchy in their intense deliberations.

The lighting of the founding fathers by the Hierarchy infused their spirits with courage and wisdom.

The magnificent wisdom of the dignity of the individual began to unfold in their hearts, and they felt deeply the responsibility for creating an unprecedented document that would rule this newfound country. The task was a great challenge.

Stubborn, recalcitrant delegates began to feel in their conscious minds what their higher selves were attempting to inject into their lower thought forms. Using the raw material from coarse matter to develop greatness requires much spiritual energy.

The leaven among the bread created Godly men and women who set up law as designed on the spiritual plane, by which they could exercise their heritage. The U.S. Constitution was a most powerful document, giving humanity their rightful heritage that had not come to the earth plane in eons of time, not since space brothers and sisters brought "The World" to Egypt, Atlantis, and Lemuria in the dim recesses of humanity's occupation on Earth had there been such universal truth.

What the sons and daughters of God had done before, they came to do again.

United Nations

Nations of the world are discovering that in their uniqueness they have something to contribute to the common good of the world. As did the Founding Fathers of the United States, so must the members of the United Nations rise above their limited nationalistic objectives, and come to stand for greatness for the common cause of evolution throughout the Earth. It calls for a magnificent demonstration of recognition of one soul—one mind—above nationalism into a true universal attitude of inter-national cooperation and altruism.

Expansion of human consciousness with common purposes has brought about the organization of a world group with planetary ideals in the United Nations body. The mere existence of such a worldwide group gives knowledge that humanity recognizes the need to come together to openly discuss differences and stress their commonality.

The U.N. is a movement toward the ideal that collectively the minds of people can solve the problems of the world. A few leaders understand decisions must be taken out of the context of emotionalism. The idea is gaining ground among responsible leaders that humanity is responsible for and to all peoples, especially when delegated a position of trust in representing the lives of their own peoples. We must rise above the motives of nationalism, and discontinue the use of physical force in any dimension.

Certain specialized agencies of the United Nations represent some of the most potentially positive groups on the world scene today. These agencies are concerned with human and natural development, aid to the less privileged, and show cooperation in trying to meet these challenges, yet are seldom mentioned in world news media.

The time is upon us when recognition of our common heritage, one soul, one source, one center of human consciousness, is a fact, not a theory. The personality and the soul of a nation, as in man, identifies itself on the mental plane. Nations must first examine Truth in collective group masterminds so that unity in diversity shall ultimately make us free.

Small Groups Forming World-wide

After two devastating world wars, the technical capability of annihilating ourselves has sobered advanced thinkers everywhere. The common man and woman throughout our globe wants permanent peace, a true sharing, and sincere fellowshipping with one another.

Because of the innate potential of planetary sister/brotherhood and imminent oneness, small groups fostering these ideals are forming all over the world.

The recognition that humanity is an energy force field of their individuality has brought recognition that groups and nations possess the same dynamic energy collectively.

Science and religion will want to see our planetary energy sources used to bring wholeness in humankind's dealings with one another.   This collective state of consciousness is being expanded to the world scene. Spirit and matter are becoming a total global concern for the first time in civilization's known history due to expansive technological and scientific advancement.

We are all to help lay the foundations of a new master plan for the evolution of humanity on planet Earth.

We will be associated in the ensuing transitional period, and closely involved in a tremendous spiritual plan that is destined to be of great blessing to the human race.

Groups serve many purposes but their members usually have a common overriding bond in some manner that draws them together.   Whether it is for only two or a hundred reasons, ideas and beliefs of people draw them together for definite purposes. The movement of groups, their ideals and goals, have progressed dramatically in the last fifty years.

Groups universally inclined all over the world are invoking the light, which is converting this darkness into light, because of the projection of light energy on the inner and outer levels of consciousness.

A.R.E. – Edgar Cayce

One of the best known groups with world-wide membership is the Association for Research and Enlightenment, whose headquarters are at Virginia Beach, Virginia.

Edgar Cayce, perhaps the world's best known psychic, gave over 14,000 life readings over a forty-year period, all documented. They were spiritual as well as physical readings dealing with health and past lives. In his sleep trance, Mr. Cayce went directly to the Akashic Records where he explored past lives. His readings revealed information of the history of man, as well as the activities and incarnation of universal consciousness in various Messiahs.

The Akashic Records are like spiritual movie screens in the ethers, upon which is imprinted the total experiences of every human being that has been upon the earth plane, and upon other planets and planes of spirit. Nothing is ever lost, for life is energy and energy is never lost. It changes form but is always present in some manner.

Those whose vibrations can tune in to the records can examine them for edification of one's enlightenment. It is not a secret to be revealed to only a few. The information is available to any vibration who is attuned to this facet of universal energy.

Cayce's information has shed light on the human-divine nature and its physical development. As a result, the A.R.E. Association was established to carry on his work.

Study groups all over the world encounter great truths as taught in the two "Search for God" books that were developed by a group of members who meditated and received guidance from the Christ for eleven years through Edgar Cayce. While in trance, Edgar Cayce prophesied that these two books would eventually be taught along with the scriptures in the New Age. Mr. Cayce's information from the Christ stated that the simple teachings he promoted 2,000 years ago had been so misunderstood He must bring light back to the true message.

Mr. Cayce dearly loved the Master Jesus, personifying His teachings. Teaching such as:

Perhaps sixty books have been written about the strange and unusual powers of this remarkable man, Edgar Cayce. His readings in health and philosophy are practiced at the A.R.E. Clinic in Phoenix, Arizona, whose founders studied the holistic health readings of Mr. Cayce. Thousands of people have been helped through the A.R.E. Foundation and the clinic.

Edgar Cayce's readings encouraged people to dedicate their lives to developing higher spiritual qualities so they could partake of the joys of the coming New Age. He gave much information about Lemuria and Atlantis, and the reasons for their disappearance. He gave information about the pyramids and the mystery schools of ancient civilizations that have been substantiated by other findings. The Foundation has been searching for the Hall of Records in Egypt which contains ancient records of humanity's history upon the Earth.

Other Groups

Findhorn Foundation

Places like the famous Findhorn Foundation in Scotland have brought worldwide attention.

Its group members have worked with the devas—the nature spirit kingdom—to bring forth a community of love and light. The help they received from the nature spirits has aided them to improve the barren soil of the windy peninsula against the North Sea, and to produce food scarcely matched anywhere else in the world.

They have learned from the Hierarchy the rules of spiritual law that have brought deep and lasting strength, and new awareness of their divine natures. They have passed on such energies to countless visitors coming from far and near to partake of their plentiful bounty.

Planetary Citizens

Planetary Citizens, whose headquarters in the United Nations Plaza in New York City, is an organization that also supports the New Age consciousness. It encourages the development of the United Nations into a truly effective, worldwide body. They encourage people to act on their convictions and spread the Word, no matter where one lives, where they work, or their particular group membership.

Uranda

In the 1930's, a young man known as "Uranda" had a vision and a call to render a ministry of love and light to his fellow man. The Emissaries of Divine Light, as they are named, have 200 Light Centers, all self-supporting, throughout the world. International headquarters were established at Sunrise Ranch near Loveland, Colorado. Canadian headquarters are at 100 Mile House, British Columbia.

Special training classes relating to the design of humankind and their purpose on Earth have been developed. For eight years, they have conducted a worldwide "Human Unity" conference. They state, "The time has come for us to join together in the process of transformation and in the restoration of the Earth."

They have established the "Foundation of Universal Unity," an educational non-profit corporation. Their purpose is to unify the thousands of people who are experiencing a state of wholeness and an awareness of global relatedness. The foundation provides local and international gathering points for many individuals and groups. The primary action of anyone associated with the foundation is to be the point of harmony, balance, at-onement in any situation. They are reaching thousands of lives throughout the world.

Order of the Round Table

The Order of the Round Table, an international brother-hood for young people of all races and creeds, assists children in their inner development through the use of symbols.

Symbolism is the art of putting into tangible form truths which have no form. Symbols touch the heart directly, bypassing the intellect, thus enabling children to become more in tune with what they already know intuitively.

Its spiritual traditions come from the beautiful legends of King Arthur and his Knights, and of all great heroes of East and West. These traditions are a reflection of ancient ceremonies which have existed to create a recognition of the unity of all people and all living things. The children are also encouraged to grow through creative work and community service.

Educo School

Another group guided by the Emissaries is the Educo School—meaning "to draw forth."

They have recognized the need for the training of the youth of our world. It has been the bent of education to pour knowledge into students rather than to let the innate beauty of the individual have an opportunity to express itself in its individual uniqueness.

The Educo School works with youth from the standpoint of leadership, recognizing the potential within the students to manifest the integrity of spirit in an outward, wholesome way that shall build a strong leadership—a mark of great leadership everywhere.

The leaders of the school themselves live this inner integrity, and serve as examples of the purity and integrity spiritual leaders in general must have for the New Age that is coming into being.

Rainbow Papers

Another avenue being explored is the possibility of implementing a publication under the name of Rainbow Papers that, in brief, will be designed to afford groups an opportunity to share their own published materials with a wider audience, to encourage creative writing that will support the child in quest for higher consciousness, and to print new materials that might otherwise remain unpublished.

Plans are underway for a series of monthly lessons that will be sent directly to the child. These lessons will center around the idea of "demonstrable truths proven through the active participation in the reality rather than the illusion of life."

Unity-in-Diversity Council

Unity in Diversity Council in Los Angeles, California, has developed a model for international and inter-group cooperation.

The Council is a worldwide coordination body of organizations, networks, and individuals seeking to "foster the emergence of a new universal peace an civilization based on unity-in-diversity among all peoples." Its work is being designed to continue the ideals and activities undertaken by six of these organizations during International Cooperation Year, voted into being for 1965 by the General Assembly of the United Nations.

As the Council concept has evolved, it has become more and more conscious of its direction toward becoming a "People's United Nations." Their valuable work began with an Annual World Festival and Directory, but it has since come to include:

1) a general assembly through which organizations, networks, and individuals can work together to solve the many problems that confront the human race;

2) specialized councils, each of which can be developed to include all interested parties; and

3) geographic councils, which encourage intergroup endeavors to be cultivated in every part of the world, as sufficient change of consciousness has taken place to call for a gathering of energies.

The term "synergy" is most applicable to the Unity-in-Diversity Council's efforts, since it focuses on all needed fields, and the Unity-in-Diversity framework has been developed to make room for all organizations that seek to participate in the intergroup network.

Unity-in-Diversity Council is constantly taking steps to contact those parties in the United States and around the world which share its goals. Activities of the Council are aimed at making the work and ideas of these parties better known to the public as well as offering other services which are requested and supported.

Spiritual Unity of Nations

One of the visions today that was first brought to the earth plane by the Masters of Wisdom in the dawn of man's beginning is the Spiritual Unity of Nations—S.U.N. Conceived by a few people of higher spiritual vision representing unity-motivated philosophy and religions, this idea burst forth to flower again initially in the hearts of a few dedicated believers.

The plan may be described as coming from a pool of wisdom, a thought reservoir established by Hierarchy, inspired by the Godhead. There are those sensitive souls who have delved into this pool of wisdom, whose minds have been impressed with those universal unity concepts, and have manifested them in concrete forms. These souls are becoming magnets of energy, focal points for the birthing again of the idea of unifying nations on a spiritual level.

The universe is governed by basic spiritual principles which are the creation of the Source or Supreme Being. The plan for the Spiritual Unity of Nations, as for any great spiritual endeavor conceived by humanity, originated in the higher planes.

For such a plan to be implemented on the material, or third-dimensional plane, it must be perceived and acted upon by someone who is receptive to the impulses from the subtler realms. There have been many adepts throughout history who have heard the call from Spirit, and many more who are awaiting their awakening to fulfill their part of the plan.

Alice Bailey called the source of this higher plan the Hierarchy. The work of the Hierarchy of the planet involves the development of self consciousness in all beings, the development of consciousness in the lower three kingdoms (mineral, vegetable, and animal), and the implementation of the will of the Planetary Logos.

The will of the Planetary Logos is primarily concerned with promoting and fostering the spirit of sister/brotherhood in humanity. This spirit has begun to seep into the consciousness of many individuals and will soon reach a critical mass.

S.U.N. Objectives

The Spiritual Unity of Nations was conceived by the Hierarchy to achieve the goals of peace and harmony on Earth. A unifying spirit of love, understanding, and tolerance must be developed and grown within humanity to carry out this plan, for which the objectives are three-fold:

1. Political – to develop and establish international consciousness in which it is recognized that all are members of the human family and have basic human rights as their birthright.

2. Religious – to establish a better world-wide understanding and consciousness of the nature of the subjective realms and tolerance among philosophies.

3. Scientific – to coordinate the activities of those in the scientific community to share scientific discoveries for the benefit of all humanity.

This plan for spiritual unification does not imply forfeiture of personal religious affiliation. Rather, it seeks to bring together people of different faiths in a spirit of tolerance and cooperation for the purpose of creating a better world in which to live.

All of the great illumined teachers who have come to the planet—Buddha, Krishna, Jesus, Muhammad, to name a few—have taught the basic principles which are embodied by the Spiritual Unity of Nations. This guiding principle is a unifying love that embraces all philosophies and can be invoked with the following prayer:

> Oh, Light of God,
> Illumine our minds –
> Oh, Love of God,
> Fill our hearts –
> Oh, Power of God,
> Direct our will –
> Let Light, Love, Power enlighten humanity.

The Birth of S.U.N.

The S.U.N. plan was brought here by the first initiates who came to Earth to help their unenlightened brothers and sisters for civilization to understand the practical reasons for unity in active expression.

In 1952, a thrust was made to plant again the Spiritual Unity concept, but it did not find fertile enough ground. Illuminated minds received ideas offering worldwide conferences from diversified religious leaders, eager to pass the vision on to activists who have the quality, power, and energy to implement it into an active reality. The time is now ripe again for the activation of the S.U.N. seed thought by each of us becoming the Light of the World.

Years ago, the S.U.N. concept was introduced to the United Nations by the Sun Centre representative from South Africa.   The U.N. has representation of many other worthwhile agencies, such as health and welfare, transportation, labor, and finance, so why not an agency to represent the spiritual groups of the world?   The U.N. leaders inferred this concept wouldn't work, and then proceeded to show the S.U.N. representative a large chart on how the U.N. functions.   In the left-hand corner was a symbol of the Sun.

No one could explain why it was there.   The smiling face seemed to be saying, "Carry on.   Some day the source of eternal light will be recognized.   One day you will recognize the sun."   Many years later this same smiling sun symbol is seen on letters, bumper stickers, and communications of all sorts.   "Have a good day," it extols.   On a higher consciousness level, energy is projecting into human consciousness that it will indeed be a good day when the U.N. includes an agency representing the spiritual groups of the world.

Most of those early S.U.N. visionaries of the 1950's are gone.   In the 1950's, people were eager to put the devastating war far behind them, to accumulate material and financial security.   Worldwide spiritual centers, where spiritual leaders of the world could come together to anchor the peace, did not interest them.

The collective wisdom of such a group could have presented their findings to show politicians, who held the reins of authority in the U.N.   They could have acted as advisors.   In this capacity, the Hierarchy could have used the enlightened ones and inspired the politicians on a positive course of action to unity and peace.   The world's resources would have been used to develop a tangible manifestation for this high purpose.

Founded by Hamid Bey

The seed for the establishment of the Spiritual Unity of Nations (S.U.N.) germinated within the mind of Coptic Fellowship International's founder, Hamid Bey, nearly 78 years ago.   Hamid Bey was trained in the ancient Mystery tradition in Egypt which he brought with him when he immigrated to the United States in the 1920's. These teachings became the foundation for Coptic Fellowship International. However, Bey's work in establishing the Coptic organization occupied so much of his time that he had to leave the development of S.U.N. to Joseph Busby in Capetown, South Africa, which Joseph began in 1952.

S.U.N., in spite of its painfully slow birthing, was established as a non-profit organization on November 11, 1982.

The first S.U.N. Conference was held in Chicago, Illinois, in 1982. It showcased presenters dedicated to assisting those on the spiritual path. In 1983 and 1984, additional conferences were held again in Chicago, and then in 1985, Estes Park, Colorado, hosted the conference, which had changed its agenda to include audience participation rather than strictly lecture presentations. In subsequent years, S.U.N. conferences were held in many cities around the nation.

In March, 1984, S.U.N. sponsored a tour to Egypt with the intention of linking East-West, inner-outer philosophies and wisdom, and then in September of that year, S.U.N. invited leaders of metaphysical and peace groups to join together in a World Unity Forum in Colorado Springs to seek ways to promote world unity. This first meeting saw the adoption of the motto "Dedicated to the Vision of the World as One Family," and provided the attending organizations the opportunity to become acquainted with each other.

The second Forum was held in January 1985 in North Carolina and it was here that the Forum's spiritual declaration of independence called "A Declaration for United Humanity" was authored.

At the last World Unity Forum in January, 1988, it was decided by consensus that each group could best serve the vision as set forth in previous Forums by working in their respective organizations in the promotion of the vision of unity among all people, and the forum format was discontinued. This, however, did not end S.U.N.'s work in the promotion of world unity and world peace.

Additional efforts included S.U.N.'s invitation to the 191 leaders of Earth's nations to attend the "Healing of the Nations" S.U.N. Conference in West Palm Beach, Florida, in January, 1990. As part of its educational initiative, S.U.N. also sponsored a tour to Arthurian England and Rennes-Le-Chateau, France, with the intent to study the implications for synthesis of the past with the future in pursuit of global peace and unity.

In 1992, a S.U.N. think tank was established and met on two occasions with the intention of refocusing and expanding S.U.N.'s active role in the world. These efforts have been ongoing, and presently S.U.N. continues to explore new ideas and ways to promote world unity and peace at the practical level.

S.U.N. Ideology

The Spiritual Unity of Nations serves as an instrument for unity. The S.U.N. serves other organizations with the sole objective of coming together in harmony for purposes of sharing perspectives of truth. This affords each participating group the opportunity to broaden its perspective without sacrificing its individual mission and principles. The S.U.N. ideology emphasizes the importance of diversity and personal choice.

Beyond these basic tenets, the S.U.N.'s creed states:

In 1981, the apparition of the Virgin Mary appeared to three children in Medjugorje, Yugoslavia. She reportedly told them that in God there are no religions and no divisions between people, that men have made the divisions that exist. Therefore it is "men," or humanity, which must remove those divides. We must adopt a creed that transcends religion. Harold Sherman in his The Green Man and His Return advocated the following statement of faith which has universal and non-sectarian appeal and would well serve as a creed for all.

I Believe

In One God, Father [Mother] of All –

In One Humanity – Every [Hu]Man my Brother [Sister]!

In One Common Freedom of Thought and Expression – Established Among All Races and Nations!

In One World – of Unity and Cooperation!

In One Purpose – Mutual Love and Understanding!

To the end that All May Attain One Great Goal in Life– Universal Peace and Happiness!

S.U.N. Objective

Citizens of the world should realize the whole universe is coordinated and activated according to a universal plan Unification of humanity is the future focal point for this planet. The Spiritual Unity of Nations has this objective:

TO ASSIST THE SHARING AND UNIFYING OF PHILOSOPHIES AND RELIGIONS FOR THE EVENTUALITY OF A SPIRITUALLY UNITED NATIONS.

In order to implement the ideal, the Spiritual Unity of Nations is dedicated to the following courses of action:

1. To bring together the efforts of all spiritually dedicated groups for the establishing of a spiritual bond between established philosophies.

2. To cooperate with leaders of religions and philosophies stressing spiritual unity and world peace.

3. To serve unity-motivated groups by providing coordinating services for cooperative effort.

4. To promote annual conferences in various world centers for the purpose of drawing together spiritual leaders of all faiths for the planning and implementation of world cooperation and harmony.

5. To provide facilities where leaders in diversified fields of service may gather and contribute their ideas and concepts to spiritual unity.

6. To seek a common bond through right thinking, right feeling, and right acting with cooperating groups encouraging collective research into fields of science, mind, health, and related research.

7. Based upon universal spiritual laws and principles, to seek every possible mode of transcending limitations that hinder the spiritual unification of humanity, and revealing solutions to problems that beset humanity.

The organizers of S.U.N. have said:

"Our focus of attention must ever be inward, upward, and forward, toward a progressive realization of a universal ideal.

"When we become aware of our personal responsibility and oral accountability to our planet as a whole, take the next step of dedication to the application of our collective knowledge, then our lives will conform to standards of truth, justice, and equality.

"We can become 'living lamps to guide the feet of humanity' and recognize that the establishment of worldwide sister/brotherhood has not only a scientific basis, but it is a fundamental basic principle relating us to nature, our planet, and the central sun around which our Earth revolves. Herein lies the test of our universality."

The formulation of this seed thought was proposed in 1952 at the S.U.N. conference in Capetown, South Africa, developed into the 60's and has come into fertilization now. Hierarchy had been impregnating individual minds with the idea, finally getting through the souls who want to see the world unified.

The Spiritual Unity of Nations transcends all limited concepts of religions. Individuals must put their focus upon God rather than upon a personality of a Buddha, a Krishna, a Jesus, or a Muhammad. The weakness of focusing on a personality, as important as it may be, opens a window for personal worship, but closes the door to any other consideration for other avenues of truth and enlightenment, leading to recognition of our common heritage.

Each one of the great avatars has previously promoted universal teachings. But humankind, in their lack of comprehending the seed of greatness residing within, began to worship the messenger, and forgot each avatar's message of universality. Previous avatars, in their own way, were working toward the goal of the Spiritual Unity of Nations.

S.U.N. Code of Ethics

> Recognition of the Light in all.
> Respect for each being.
> Respect for earth, air, and water.
> Respect for plants and animals.
> Respect for space and all life.

S.U.N. Movement

The Spiritual Unity of Nations—the S.U.N.—is a major emphasis of the second stage of the World Light return.

The S.U.N. movement is twofold, both exoteric (outer), and esoteric (inner). The exoteric symbol of the S.U.N. is expressed through that great cosmic intelligence known as the Solar Logos—the Lord of the Sun—of which the physical sun is but his outer garment, and the inner spheres are his inner garments.

This is a work which is a projection, a seed concept of this great consciousness, interpreted to meet the needs of humanity as they move into the new Aquarian dispensation.

The sun energies hold within their radiance a cosmic plan.   There is nothing disorderly about this evolving procedure. From the very birth of this solar system—which is a comparatively small one on the outer fringe of the Milky Way—the great Lord of the Sun, who took his place in this portion of the universe, appointed selected representatives of the solar hierarchy to be responsible for the spiritual life of the planets.

Each planet is in a process of developing in its own particular way. The Earth planet has evolved to the stage where human beings can be clothed in garments of flesh and form and experience, personality awareness, and an outer physical coat encasing the essence of light.

The great spiritual hierarchy has, gradually through the ages, unfolded one aspect of the plan after another through appointed representatives, and so the great spiritual traditions and philosophical systems have been established.

And now comes the time for a new vision, and one of the new visions reflects the S.U.N.—Spiritual Unity of Nations. Can we not sense here the use of the word "sun" as the symbol of universal light? The S.U.N. of God, the sun, the light of God, and the light and sun spirit within all people everywhere will assimilate accelerated Aquarian energies. Each of us become the Light of the World, which indicates a future of positivity and peace on Earth.

The Coptic Fellowship and members representing many other spiritual organizations are reflecting the vision of the Spiritual Unity of Nations, recommending their own spiritual recognition, and a U.N. spiritual agency as such, be developed within the structure of the United Nations.

Spiritual vision is brought into focus in the United Nations, as it becomes pro-truth, pro-unity for sister/brotherhood, for enlightenment. The concepts of universality go beyond the individualized interpretation of personal interests and develops a broadly divine interpretation.

Coptic Fellowship

As enlightenment came to individuals and small groups throughout the world, so the inner hunger for more awareness grew. Meeting together in small light groups of fellowship, to seek guidance, to hear the story of unfoldment in others, brought courage and strength of belief.

The esoteric began to gain favor as individuals discovered their own latent powers. They began to tell of personal unfolding in song and prose. The demand for further knowledge continues to increase, for it strikes a response in the streams of memory for humankind.

We belong to a new humanity, born again beyond personality, beyond soul, born again to a Universal Awareness. We should not be concerned with creating a new religion. We are not interested in establishing another organization.

We simply want messengers of the Great Light embracing all religions.

The Great Age has started and unification of souls is the challenge of the day.

At last, the Universal Vision appears!

They are waiting for a message. They are waiting for a messenger, and that is the Spiritual Unity of Humanity.

Be pro the truth, and give no place in your thinking for negative or anti-anything.

Be pro the great light.

Be pro the God Power and be as positive and direct as humanly possible.

As Christ said, know these are the children of the light.

Lay current foundations. To move forward for us to have Light of your First Master, which is our soul self.

Rejoice at our inner awakening for where there is awakening, there is freedom, and freedom is heaven.

Freedom is the Spirit. All else binds, so we must have unity with a promise of freedom. We will become free and liberated souls, not bound by anyone or anything.

The new message is one of illumination. There is no limit to the levels we may attain if we dedicate ourselves to the work required.

The Coptic Fellowship teaches that spiritual development is attained through a daily practice of diet, exercise, meditation, and self-mastery.

The more we follow the principles of healthy living and selfless service, the higher we rise in consciousness, even to the point of God Consciousness.

Thank God our time has come. The challenge is an adventure into God. The Great God Power has broken through.

Humanity must have the courage and expenditures to educate the youth of the world.

But educate them to what? To lead them simply into knowledge that the right human relations are vital to a peaceful world.

People need to talk about universality rather than differences and boundaries. Peace and goodwill must be taught and applied by all, everywhere. If spiritually-oriented people become dynamically active worldwide, and totally committed to excellence and universal love, the belief systems of the world would change dramatically to positive courses of action.

The Coptic Fellowship provides 5 different types of training—the World Service Order training, Teacher training, Self-Mastery training, Ministerial training, and Youth education.

World Service Order

Since 1985, the World Service Order has trained hundreds of leaders who have found their way to inspire others. Many are now leading their own organizations, while others are travelling nationally, giving lectures and workshops.

World Service Order Leadership Training is a 4-weekend commitment to growth, development and finding your personal path of service. WSO has two objectives:

1. How to create a better you, a better community and a better world.
2. Teaches practical principles of leadership. Preparing individuals to expand their level of service.

Sessions are a combination of workshops, lectures, and sensitivity training with facilitators who have all been graduates of the World Service Order program. Students learn to prepare and deliver professional and inspiring presentations, gain confidence, and feel empowered to serve.

Participants will find within themselves their personal role of service for their group and community. Many find their role as world servers in WSO; for others, it is also the first level of training necessary to move into Coptic Teacher Training. Information on this course will be available at the Conference.

Coptic Teacher Training

Having completed World Service Order training, candidates may elect to move into Coptic Teacher Training.

The basic objective of Teacher Training is to learn about the Coptic Fellowship, and develop the ability to pass that knowledge on to others. Teacher candidates are taught the ancient history of the Coptics, and the modern tenets and beliefs of the Coptics.

As a second objective of the year, students are taught how to move into their hearts. In an atmosphere of mutual trust, friendship, respect and love, we all share our inner and outer truth together.

Subjects covered include:
1. History of the Coptics
2. Advanced metaphysical theory
3. Advanced meditation techniques
4. Subconscious reprogramming techniques
5. Publicity – How to create a promotional brochure and use the media to attract people to events.

Self-Mastery Training

Self-Mastery Training is a course to be attended after Coptic Teacher Training. It is designed to allow participants to put into practice Coptic Self-Mastery as presented by Master Hamid Bey.

All true development must come from within. To grow in any aspect one must recognize his/her own responsibility in promoting personal growth.

We all possess hidden and secret powers—powers of mind, body and spirit. We are not consciously aware of these powers, and rarely use them. In Self-Mastery training students learn, step by step, what powers they need to develop, and exactly how to develop them.

This includes a daily practice of:
1. Breathing Exercises
2. Concentration
3. Meditation
4. Proper Nutrition

5. Being aware of how we treat others and ourselves
6. Learning to see, hear and respond as a Master
7. Being aware of how our mind and our thoughts impact our "true" selves, and others.

Students of the Self-Mastery Training program learn to develop and cultivate these powers and use them in their daily lives to ensure healthier bodies, stronger minds, greater poise, peace, happiness, and ultimate success.

Coptic Ministerial Training

Ministerial Training may be taken by those who have successfully completed World Service Order training, Teacher Training, and the Self Mastery Program. Coptic Ministers represent the Light Ministry of Coptic Fellowship International.

The symbol associated with the Light Ministry is the Ankh. The Ankh in ancient Egyptian times was known as the "key of life."

Ministerial candidates learn techniques of successful living. They learn how to perform the services of an Ordained Minister, including worship services, weddings, funerals, and baptisms.

Minister Training teaches spiritual counseling, tools to facilitate seminars, trains candidates how to run their own unique centers, and develop their individual ministry. In addition, they will have opportunities to further develop their speaking, leadership, and organizational skills.

Coptic Children's Program

The Coptic Fellowship is advocating a children's program dedicated to the spiritual nurturing of the child. Created in an atmosphere of love, humility, and service, this children's program recognizes the common thread of truth inherent in and transcending all world teachings, and seeks to work in harmony with other New Age groups.

This concerted effort for the education of the child has a focal point of light that reaches out to touch the lives of many kindred souls who diligently work to bring insight, understanding, and revelation to a weary world. Coptics ask us to merge our light with thousands of other "lights" striving to merge in attainment to create a brilliance on this planet that will illuminate minds and hearts everywhere.

The Coptic children's program seeks to help the child realize his/her full potential as a spiritual being. Children possess an innate ability to love. They are gifted with intuition and they are still immeasurably close to their source of illumination. It is time for each child to become more fully aware of his own inner "light."

It is the Coptic Fellowship's aspiration to:
1. Stir the hearts of those who envision universal harmony and oneness between all peoples, religions, and nations.
2. Establish a gathering place where ideas, materials, and concepts may be assembled, and then collectively shared with others who choose to serve the child.
3. Provide a reservoir of thought consciousness to inspire individuals and groups to originate new materials and techniques to teach the child.

They only hope to achieve these collective goals through a cooperative exchange of ideas, each light group retaining its own identity.

You Are Called

Every enlightened son and daughter is getting a perspective of spiritual truth, as they work together beautifully. Only by combined effort and unity of thought can civilization bring forth the teachings that will pave the way for the return of the Light of the World.

Disciples of this universal unity plan sense the divine purpose for its unfolding. Each disciple—representing different religious bents—takes on a special task, according to the volunteering of personal talents for ensuring the plan ultimately develops. Each facet of the great plan has unique requirements. Disciples worldwide will learn to work with the plan through their personalized practical service and experience.

The few dedicated universalists in the world today are bypassing self-serving political structures and social organizations who have little capacity for unified vision. The universalists are reaching out to the business community, the farmers, the housewives, and the carpenters who want to see their children grow up in a world of peace and opportunity, fulfilling their dreams on all levels of expressions.

This plan for unity is subject to adaptation too evolved for the conformists. In general terms, its primary objective is to unify humanity into one subjective but diversified whole—an idealistic dream, but within our collective reach, because of the individual birthing of the Light of the World and its expansion eventually into a universal mastermind.

The corporate body spearheading S.U.N. comes from unified diversities, the molding of talents on many levels of endeavor. The concept is all-encompassing and perhaps without precedent, but its seeds have been planted in fertile consciousness. To attain this vision of unity of all nations, representing all colors, all races, into one huge instrument, requires a unifying spirit of love, understanding, and mutual tolerance, a true expression of unity in diversity.

All those who worked together for the great cause, came to inspire humanity and to spiritualize all life on this planet.

Our elder brothers who have watched over us lifetime after lifetime, age after age, have called us to this high purpose. The great teachers in high places pour their great love upon humanity, for our cause is their cause and their cause is our cause.

Let the past be past. Let us enter into a new day of everlasting light.   Everlasting day, everlasting truth, everlasting. Take claim to the great promise of Christ to those who accepted his vision in bygone days. "I come that ye may have life, and have it more abundantly."

And remember, we are not alone. We may at times feel alone, but we are never alone. "I am with you always, even to the end of the world."

That is the cosmic call, the voice divine, seeking to manifest his presence through us, and then our voice will be the voice of God. Our ears will hear the divine melody. Our thoughts will be the thoughts of God. Our hearts will radiate love divine, an outpost of the divine in human form, fulfilling his own purpose. What a glorious and wonderful challenge! What a beautiful awakening! We will walk together tomorrow and tomorrow and tomorrow—and all the eternal tomorrows, to the greater glory of God.

We Are All Responsible

Personal and group responsibility must be assumed by humankind to direct their behavior toward perfection, both inward and outward.

One does not perpetrate their carelessness upon their family or their neighbor. One must constantly ask the question of themselves, "Does what I think or do cause any wrong to my fellow beings?" If so, then it must not be done.

The act of love brings good universally to all of humanity. The law of universal unconditional love is the supreme law. Humanity should realize their responsibility in understanding and obeying the laws of love, so ultimately there will exist a unity of purpose and understanding of operation of law before group energy can bring about peace and harmony in its particular area of responsibility.

When love reigns supreme, there is a yielding, a compromising of purpose. No deep difference of individuality will exist to mar relationships as group cooperation brings harmony into the world of form.

Accepting Our Personal Responsibility as a Light of the World

This world service opportunity manifested on the birth date of the Mayan prophecy, December 21, 2012, and reenergized on January 1, 2013. These historic prophetic dates mean "the light of the world" when the chosen illuminating WORLD SERVERS assume their responsibility as a LIGHT OF THE WORLD.

Each LIGHT OF THE WORLD is asked to take their personal time every day to pray for a better world. Every day is a birth date and a conception date. Nine months after every conception date, a potential birth could be realized as a result of the appointed LIGHT OF THE WORLD prayer for a better world for everyone on the planet.

Win-Win is the goal of our collective prayers. As we know, our Earth sun shines down on all of creation—the birds, animals, fish, and peoples of all nations and religions. Our responsibility as a LIGHT OF THE WORLD is to pray for all creation on Earth, all peoples of all nations and religions.   All men and women are created equal and to repeat—Win-Win is always our goal as a LIGHT OF THE WORLD.

The 33rd degree of masonry was revered by the U.S. founding fathers during the formation of our country July 4, 1776.   Remarkably, the power of universal love for all peoples of all nations was energized on January 1, 2013. Each year since the beginning of time has had a life lesson to express. The planetary life lesson of January 1, 2013, is the 33rd degree of masonry, encompassing the vision of all peoples on Earth living in world peace, world unity, and world prosperity.

Each of us is a co-creator with the Supreme Creator to assist this planetary shift. We create by the nature of our thoughts, words, and deeds. Every person has the capacity to help change the world. All it takes is intentional effort to manifest the world we desire.

Each of us can, with proper intent and motivation, take responsibility for the nature and quality of our thoughts, and the proper care of the Earth, over which we have stewardship. If each of us chooses to care for our fellow human beings who are less fortunate than ourselves in a spirit of philanthropy, we could collectively help eliminate suffering and want among the human family. These are realistic and achievable goals.

A simple daily regimen of meditation, prayer, and practical action in whatever form suits you—volunteerism, environmental activism, or other humanitarian endeavors— is all that is required to recreate the world. It does require discipline and the willingness to encourage others to do the same, for manifestation works best when the participants are great in number.

Every person on the planet who responds to the inner desire to serve in some fashion is a part of this group of World Servers. The contribution of each person is very significant within the collective.

Our responsibility is to encourage as many planetary light servers to pray every day and think as big as possible with positive thought projections to ensure that that birth date of our new 26,000-year time period is powerfully positive on the physical, mental, emotional, and spiritual dimensions.

All peoples of all religions and all nations will benefit from this birth of a new 26,000-year time period is powerfully positive on the physical, mental, emotional, and spiritual dimensions. All peoples of all religions and all nations will benefit from this birth of a new 26,000-year time period.

If you share this planetary vision, please feel free to share this book with your family and friends. It will be through the expression of the LIGHT OF THE WORLD that readied men and women shall again be shown the true power of the LIGHT OF THE WORLD and show the way to a positive future for planet Earth.

Through the power of prayer, invocation, and creative visualization, we can unite in peace, for the healing of the races, for the healing of the nations. Use meditation and prayer in service to the planet and humanity. The important thing is to practice with the proper intent and purity of motivation, and to do it daily. A few minutes a day is all it takes to change the world.

Birthing of the World Light

Much will be written about the birthing of the World Light within the individual.

The winds of promise are sweeping across the mountains and the plains of all lands. In every place upon the planet there are sons and daughters of God sharing their spiritual experience, usually in twos and threes, some by the tens and twenties, and a few by the hundreds.

Many souls are at the point of searching for the Christ outwardly in the group situation, still hungering, not recognizing individual responsibility to become still and let the Christ birth occur. But in small group gatherings, those who have anchored the Light within their own beings are increasing this light, magnifying it a thousandfold through light projection, meditation, singing and silence, the inner communion with their higher selves.

Their expressions of joy and thanksgiving are feeding the newness of discovery among the yet-unchallenged searchings of the Light. This nurturing has brought fruition in the hearts of the foundlings, bringing them into maturity of feeling and expression that has permitted them to go out with courage to announce to the world their newfound joy.

The World Light Consciousness finally is now proliferating and uniting instead of fracturing and diminishing.

The birth of a major planetary cycle has arrived. The planetary light workers are being called to plant mental and spiritual seeds for the future of planet Earth.

According to the Mayan calendar, December 21, 2012, marked the beginning of a new 26,000- year cycle. A scientific analysis shows that the birthdate of this new 26,000-year time period has a high potential to be very positive on all levels for the future of humanity.

Included below are two suggested prayers that you could use. Or you may use any other prayer of your choice to manifest this vision of the LIGHT OF THE WORLD. Your destiny is to become the LIGHT OF THE WORLD.

Read this prayer out loud every day.

Recommended Light of the World Prayer

Almighty Mother-Father-God, I pray for healings on all levels—physical, mental, emotional, and spiritual—in all families, in all hospitals & health centers, in all doctors' offices, psychologists' offices, in AA meetings, in addiction counseling sessions, and everywhere else were healing is needed and desired.

I pray that all politicians choose peace in all circumstances. (Bring Ten Commandments to national and international expression.) I pray that all of humanity remember that all children worldwide are symbolically our children, and all people are our brothers and sisters. I pray that women everywhere are empowered and experience equality with men. (All men and women are created equal.) I pray that slavery is eliminated from planet Earth. I pray that governmental laws be for the benefit "of the people, by the people, and for the people." (The hungry find food, the homeless find homes, and the sick and injured are healed.) I pray that all nations share their nation's natural resources with their people and other nations.

I pray that all religious and spiritual leaders to pray daily for all good to manifest on Earth, and they continually seek the manifestation of the peaceful coexistence and cooperation of religions. I pray that businesses succeed in a.. nations. And as a result of national and international business successes, everyone everywhere find meaningful, creative, life-sustaining work. I pray that the worldwide economy becomes the most successful and stable in the history of the planet.

The Light Prayer

By Jim Goure

I release all of my past to the Light.
I release all of my negatives to the Light.
I release all of my relationships to the Light.
I release all of my fears to the Light.
I release all of my future to the Light.
I release all of my inner self to the Light.
I release all of my human desires to the Light.
I am a Light Being.
I radiate the Light from my Light Center throughout my entire being.
I radiate the Light from my Light Center to everyone.
I radiate the Light from my Light Center to everything.
I AM in the center of a bubble of Light.
Only Light can come to me, and only Light can be here.
Thank you Creator for everyone, for everything, and for me.
Most of all, Thank You, Creator, for Thee.

Preparing to become a Light of the World

Humanity's knowledge of Earth has broadened considerably since it was first thought the Earth was flat. The planet, indicated the scientists, is millions, perhaps billions of years of age. Through archaeological studies of caves, excavations of ancient cities, fossil remains, the secrets of ancient Earth and its inhabitants are being unfolded.

If we were to depend on humanity's limited knowledge of history, not much could actually be told. However, for understanding the soul's purpose for being on Earth, the past is important. To know how the individual fits into this Great Plan, much information is needed as to human origin.

Many esoteric sources exist that lend valuable light on humanity's memory of the past—the esoteric source of Ancient Wisdom. Some of this invaluable knowledge is referred to in the Bible, whose words have been shrouded by symbology and parables, whose true esoteric meanings have in too many cases been misinterpreted.

Ancient Wisdom tells us "animal-man" appeared about twenty-one million years ago. More animal than human, he still had the physique and appearance of man.

Since the human was first in the mind of God, his first awareness was spiritual—man became a soul.

Consciousness of the Light was followed by darkness. The Scriptures say, "Darkness covered the face of the deep." The human as spirit had betrayed his heritage. Souls became involved in matter at various levels of enlightenment. Most were in darkness.

That is when God declared the human should have help in redeeming himself into the Light. Superior Beings, who had not been entrapped in physical bodies of the Earth, volunteered to come to the rescue. They were known as the White Brotherhood or Hierarchy of Masters of Wisdom.

They established headquarters on the etheric realm. This realm is known as Shamballa. Through Hierarchy's efforts, animal-man became individualized—a primitive human being. History calls them Lemurians, from the land of Lemuria—the land the Pacific Ocean presently covers. It also included parts of North and South America.

The Great White Brotherhood

The Great White Brotherhood—the "First Group" of like-minded souls—moved among humanity, being in their advanced spiritual development rulers, priests, and leaders of the less developed populace.

The gradual reawakening of the soul brought a measure of light in more advanced animal bodies.

As the evaluation of this animal-man kingdom development, souls began projecting their energy by "thought forms" into such creatures. As these thought forms crystallized, monstrosities developed. Sordid and strange creatures were created, which were eventually eliminated, disappearing by the time of the Flood.

Such stirring of principles of desire and emotion aroused primitive man to become inquisitive. He began to acquire material things that made life more and more comfortable. His mind became more fertile—eventually many inventions brought more and more pleasure. This led to excessive gratifications with low standards of living, resulting in the breakdown of spirituality the White Brotherhood had tried to promote.

The Hierarchy then decreed their members to withdraw from the Earth, and to return to etheric planes.

Although the leaders withdrew from physical involvement in humanity's affairs, they continued to be supportive on the spiritual level.

Rise of Civilization

As humans came together, common bonds of mutual love welded them into groups, no matter how alien their beliefs were from other groupings. Humanity has gone down this same path century after century. Common language and purpose continually welded nations together, isolating larger groups, creating national pride that went far beyond the limits of original purpose.

Having lost their awareness that as children of God they were rightfully entitled to their spiritual and material riches, they preyed upon neighbors from nearby localities, which resulted in national invasions of territories. This situation brought continual fear and alienation among those cultures whose mores were different from their neighbors.

Civilizations progressed in physical, mental, and spiritual powers, but as they lost their spiritual centeredness, their great glory grew dim and these self-motivated civilizations faded from the annals of history.

Merging of East and West

The simple life lived by the sages gave adequate time for contemplation, ingrained innately in the Eastern people to properly examine the inner person. The Eastern world is positive to things of the Spirit, while the Western world is positive to things material and external. This potential marriage of cultures represents a balance of polarity of energy, the Earth striving for this balance in negative and positive energy. Yet since America was designated to be the birthplace of the new Israel, the forces of spiritualization for the preparation for the return had begun to take form.

When Jesus was asked His mission, He replied, "I have come to seek and save that which is lost."

Jesus did not mean that He had come to save any soul that was lost. He knew that in God's kingdom there is no soul ever lost. It was simply the teaching of the Truth that had been lost. The WAY had been clouded symbolically by the dust and dirt-filled winds of a priesthood which knew the Truth but failed to teach its essence.

Jesus knew that His consciousness was a condition of knowing, and one which could be attained eventually by all humanity. But as He exemplified the Truths more completely than any man had yet done, He invited all humankind to do as He Himself had done.

The Christ through Jesus announced that the pattern He had created is the best and only one to use. To this end, He stated, "I AM THE WAY, THE TRUTH, AND THE LIFE. NO MAN COMETH UNTO THE FATHER BUT BY ME," simply meaning that before a soul attained God Consciousness, Christ Consciousness must be achieved. Jesus incarnated in the Messianic Role to point the Way of the Divine Road for humanity to follow.

Universal Unity

It is inherent to be in fellowship with one another. Being a spark of God in original vibration, the individual is lonely without his or her kind. To be isolated from one another prevents the development of love for their fellowmen, denying the opportunity to create soul qualities of compassion, sharing, and service.

These are necessary for a person to balance his or her karma, and to move again toward perfect union with the Source. Enlightened individuals have always guided their brothers and sisters into the light. Possessing greater awareness and wisdom by treading the path first, their love demanded serving and guiding their less developed fellow beings toward the inner spiritual home.

Because of the soul's longing to fellowship with its kind, there have been unlimited gatherings to share labor and love. When humanity developed into family groups, the bonds of family life ran deep and far throughout the Earth, anchoring light for the development of the Earth and all humankind. Families loved and fought together, but in common need, stayed together to nurture family members. Groups, as they developed, were extensions of the basic structure of the family. Hamlets, villages, and eventually, cities were repetitions of the nucleus of original groupings.

Throughout the ages philosophers have always given the same similar doctrine to the world. They have espoused that there is but One—one substance, one mind, one unitary plan throughout all creation, in all nature.

Principles may be many, but they are all derivatives of one common law. To announce a law at first, then to discuss the principles of that law, would be to give first a full-fledged premise and then try to prove the premise. This type of instruction has been made in an attempt to teach eternal verities.

We approach the thought of Unity in the "hidden One" with respect and reverence. We are on hallowed ground— our words are true and holy. We are speaking into your hearts from an appreciative and thankful spirit that God supplies the lesson of our enlightenment.

Sages throughout history have pointed out the truth that multiplicity springs forth from unity. Jesus gave the illustration by using the mustard plants from a single seed as an example. He said, "If he had the faith of a grain of mustard seed." He perceived that God-Consciousness unfolded from within. The seed knew—had absolute faith —that it had all the life there is in it, and if planted, would grow. Every principle heretofore has exposed our examination and contemplation inherent in that tiny object.

The philosopher proves that a Law of Unity exists by observing the principles of that Law. We, then, have reached this conclusion where we can proclaim Unity—the Absolute—as being all that is, in itself becoming the relative.

Only Spiritual Power Can Unite the World

Only spiritual power—Divine Love, Wisdom, Power— can unify the peoples of the world, the nations of the world.

Working into a universal direction of unity, Hierarchy is behind this objective. The Elder Brothers of the human race are working for this goal, and they had to wait till the coming of this, the Aquarian Age, before they could release these dynamic ray energies to bring about Divine Alchemy, and dispense those qualities—the new inspirations that will appeal to people everywhere—even to people who have no spiritual inclinations.

This is a universal message that will appeal to politicians, scholars, scientists, astronauts, cosmonauts, and leaders of all ideologies.

The one unifying power is to listen to the voice that is Cosmic—the voice that rings with Truth—a universal message, a global message that carries within its wings, truth and enlightenment of man as a soul.

Former centers of past civilizations are turning toward the West where the New World awaits the beginning of a

New Dispensation and a New Civilization.. A civilization is always based on a strong universal philosophy of Truth, for a strong productive center of civilization cannot survive devoid of a steadfast belief in the Divine.

When consciousness of a supreme power is cooperatively linked to earthly powers, a positive civilizing influence results. A materialistic civilization may be resurrected behind a Western civilization built by Master-building, Truth-loving minds under the divine guidance of a re-born Messianic Consciousness.

Unveiling of Truth

The unveiling of Truth is sometimes so intensified, it can be overwhelming.

Humanity finally recognizes the limitation of its finite mind, and reaches out to embrace the revelation of a larger Truth. This is when the development of the inner spiritual child begins.

First comes the revelation, the birth, then comes the development. In his innocent beginning as a new child of the Father, one may stumble and fall, yet knowing one's destiny has purpose and plan, one looks ever inward for the original blueprint of the plan. To be ashamed at his ignorance for past history is a waste of energy. The soul must move ever forward and upward, taking in power, expanding, and perpetually searching for its home.

The unfolding truth is a glorious dawning of the new-born soul. This is exhilarating, giving life purpose to a degree never experienced before. It makes one aware of fellow beings who are also struggling at different levels of understanding. One feels compassion for one's neighbor who is undergoing his or her own birthing into Christ Consciousness.

Mysticism and Intuition

The word "psychic" comes from "psyche," meaning soul, and signifies man's capacity to perceive, control, and receive knowledge beyond the well-known five senses.

Mysticism is a particular manifestation of the intuitive life.

An inner power is tapped, which can be channeled for envisioning the past or future, for healing, or communicating with persons who no longer exist on this earthly plane. It is often part of their soul development to help those still on the earth plane.

The veil is fragile that separates the Earth and the next level of advancement the soul goes to on its journey back home. It can be penetrated by spiritually and intuitionally developed individuals.

As it is on the earth plane, where each individual is at a level of development, so it is on astral and etheric planes.

The etheric level is the universal love realm. The etheric interpenetrates the entire solar system, including the physical and astral realms.

The astral realms pertain specifically to realms or planes between the physical and etheric.

The astral is a matter of vibration rather than designated areas of space. Lower astral realms are next to the earth plane level of consciousness, while higher astral levels approach the etheric—the universal love realms.

Each realm has also several levels within its structure, so there is a fusion of vibrations or levels within the entire structure of vibrational levels.

Where many frequencies of vibration exist, people can develop their consciousness to a degree that their "spiritual eyes" can perceive into the higher realms of consciousness. As long as the soul is encased in the physical garment, they can aspire to expand vision to include the levels and planes of vibration far beyond present comprehension.

We have greater opportunities to perceive these levels of being than any other period in history. Vibrating at a higher recorded intensity through attainment of light and love consciousness will be needed to elevate to this state of awareness. Now is the time!

The purpose of life is to be able to unwind the mysteries past, present, future—to blaze the trail of humanity that is to come and to have a vision that will enable one to look back and say, "I did my part!"

The Power of Words

Everything that exists, or has ever existed, began as thought.

The creation of the universe began as a thought in the mind of the Creator.

On Earth, The Egyptian Mystery Schools tell us that the first being to create by thought was Thoth. Even his name evokes the power of thought—Thot(h). According to the Dictionary of All Scriptures and Myths, Thoth "was the incarnated Thought, the living Word. . .the divine intelligence, which at the creation uttered the words that resulted in the formation of the world. He was self-produced, and was lord of earth, air, sea, and sky. He was the scribe of the gods, and the inventor of all arts and sciences."

Alice Bailey wrote of the power of the Word in "The Word of Power" wherein she described the Logos, or Creative Source, which created our solar system. From this Word (AUM) are derived countless other words, all of which are credited with the creation of the planet and the "five kingdoms of nature":

1) the Mineral
2) the Vegetable
3) the Animal
4) the Human
5) the Spiritual

It is an awesome creative power which the Word possesses. Bailey describes the origin and power of the Word as follows:

1) All the words of Power are rooted in the Great Word committed to the Solar Logos at the dawn of manifestation.

2) All the words of Power are permutations or expansions of three basic sounds, and increase in length as the planes are involved, until the sentences and speech of the finite unit—man—in their myriad differentiations are arrived at.

3) Therefore, on the path of return, speech becomes ever more brief. Words are more sparingly used, and the time eventually comes when the adept employs formulas of words only as required to carry out specific purposes along two lines.

This, of course, is on the planes in the three worlds of spirit, mind, and emotion.

4) The aspirant, therefore, has mainly these things to do when preparing for initiation:

5) Every Word affects the deva kingdoms, and hence the form-building aspects of manifestation. No sound is ever made without producing a corresponding response in every substance, and driving multitudes of tiny lives to take specific forms. The majority of human beings as yet build unconsciously, and the form constructed is either of a beneficent or maleficent agency.

A basic understanding of the power that words and, by extension, thought, have on the spiritual and mental planes is necessary before we can begin to understand how this can impact our physical lives.

All events, which occur on the physical plane, have their start in the higher (spiritual, mental, emotional) planes. This is a basic principle of manifestation, and the reason our beliefs create our reality. They have their beginning in the subtler realms, where a seed is planted by a thought, emotion, or spoken word. From there, they grow as they are given energy by repetition of the thought, emotion, or word, and eventually become manifest as physical events.

As Bailey stated, most people create unconsciously, and a great deal of damage and unnecessary trauma has been created by people creating unconsciously. Bailey wrote about this very subject more than 80 years ago. Imagine what a different world we would have if people had taken her wisdom to heart at the time of her writing. We can do something now to change our future if we so choose. This is a very simple discipline which anyone can practice with a little conscious effort.

Spiritual Progression

Since people approach God by different paths, all approaches to Truth must be synthesized. Truth is universal, and everyone is in a different classroom, as it were, to learn the lessons needed for this structural evolution as distinct from his physical evolution.

There are two evolutions side by side. To evolve means to aspire.

Naturally we have a soul link to many religions, but not to the Christ of any particular church or philosophy. The Universal Christ Spirit—Universal Light Principle—is ever seeking to manifest itself in many forms.

So it is each of us and the Great Light that ultimately counts, and in this way certain areas of our brains are activated. This cannot be done if we subconsciously slip back into the past. We have to update everything.

Self-Guided Individuals Can Contribute Most

The sort of individuals who stand on their own are guided by the light of their own soul, and are the ones who can contribute most to humanity—who can achieve the most. So firstly we have to cast off all that we sense as a hindrance. Do not try to bolster up that which is old and of the past. Look to the past as stepping stones, and an experience in spiritual growth.

Development of a person's individual soul must go hand-in-hand with one's yearning for merging with the divine. Without ultimate faith in a personal God as the True Creator and Supreme Wisdom behind every individual, there can be no "spiritual civilization" in the fullest sense of the word.

Truth has been clouded over by ages of pseudo-intellectual training, which has left humanity's minds spiritually hungry for wisdom from the high spiritual planes. Now the esoteric groups are starting to answer the needs of humankind, bringing a knowing of Truth seldom before experienced.

Ancient wisdoms are being revealed to individuals who have meditated long before their private altars in the secret place of their Most High. They have been instructed through telepathy from higher sources to spread the Word to those who were hungering for their wisdom.

Putting advanced knowledge in print has developed groups through various kinds of self-development study courses. As groups meet together, they discover the wealth of information on their long inner struggle to become truly spiritual again.

The small light group tends to support each member's growth. They are finding universal spiritual food and the hungry spiritual aspirant desires the bread of essence.

Past Lives in Present Time

We're living all our past lives simultaneously.

Anybody you're emotionally attracted to on a positive or negative level, is you from another lifetime. Because you are an electromagnetic force field. What you're attracting is YOU—a mirror of one of your past lives.

And you're given an opportunity, when you attract them, and when you recognize, particularly the Judases, what did Jesus say? "Forgive them, Father, for they know not what they do." Because you were just like them in another lifetime. It's how you handle them that determines the expansion of consciousness.

I think one of the purposes of life is how to handle difficult people. We don't want to hurt anybody. We don't want to hurt Judas at all—we realize we were just like him.

That realization will bring peace on Earth.

What we're here for is peace on Earth.

To bring forth what we came to bring forth, and when the whole energy field shifts because of your presence here, and you take the role of the big thinker—universally—embracing all religions, all nations, all peoples.

We lived in all these countries. We spoke all these languages. As soon as we come into this lifetime—just before you were born—you said, "I'm going to remember my past lives," and then you take your first breath and poof—it's all gone!

And where are you? You're with Mom and Dad! And this may be a shock to you, but they were your children in past lives! The way they treated you is the way you treated them. It's quick karma or dharma right away.

And that energy is really something, because really, you are pure light. Pure light! We don't know that. It's like having millions of dollars in the bank and not knowing you have it. It's just stored there. Millions. Tremendous light.

As soon as we hit the earth plane, we create ripples. The first ripple is Mom and Dad, because family DNA is much more powerful than you could possibly imagine.

You realize that this electromagnetic field—that parental issue—and all your relatives are so powerful. That old saying among us psychologists—the thoughts of the parents become the thoughts of the children. Heard that before?

The next ripple is your childhood. All the friends you had as a child. Then you went to high school. A whole different batch of friends. Then you get a little older and maybe went to college—all those buddies and pals and lady friends. Then you started a job—and your boss is just like you in another lifetime! The people you work with are just like you.

Remember, when you're emotionally attached— positively or negatively—and you point a finger at anyone, there are three fingers pointing back at you! Remember, don't hurt anybody! That's the key here.

Passing Life's Tests

The science of numerology reveals the specific tests we must pass in our lifetime. In this case, we look to the Sphinx to guide us. Ancient tradition says that the riddle of the Sphinx provides the meaning of life.

Each letter of the word "sphinx" represents a test we must pass before we can graduate from the earth plane. When one of these letters appear in a person's name, it represents a test that person must face in the current lifetime. The goals are self-mastery and humility.

The letter S represents the test of power, and often signifies that power was misused in a previous life, and the individual will face experiences where they are a victim of power abuse. Passing this test requires one to embody the spiritual principles of unconditional love, selfless giving, and non-judgement.

The letter P represents the test of willpower. Each test is different, and therefore successfully passing the test depends on various factors. In general, controlling one's passions, and focusing on what is good and right in each situation for all involved is the key to passing this test.

The letter H represents the money test. Those with this letter in their name often face situations in which they have limited funds and must work hard to make ends meet. In some cases, great wealth is thrust upon the individual, resulting in a very different test. Successfully passing this test requires embodying generosity, regardless of the amount of wealth possessed.

The letter I, being the word for self, naturally represents the test of ego. To pass this test, the individual must grow beyond self-centeredness and develop the habit of thinking of others first in all situations.

The letter N represents the freedom test. Many with this letter in their name feel that they have limited freedom, with too many responsibilities. Sometimes, the test involves having virtually unlimited freedom. To pass this test, the individual must find a balance between freedom and responsibility, giving each the appropriate attention.

The final letter X represents the service test. While many of the other tests require the individual to be of service to others, this test comes only after the others have been passed, and requires one to serve on a higher level, through leadership in some form. The best leaders, as we know, are those who see themselves as a servant to all.

Growth Brings Awareness

The auric vibrations of Earth itself are accelerating, causing apparent restlessness among its peoples whose vibrations are in the embryonic state of spiritual birth. Many feel out of sorts emotionally and mentally—tangible signs of the birthing process. They must raise their individual vibrations through prayer and meditation, altruistic love and service, to become harmonious with new dynamic energies.

Much regeneration must be done on all levels of the world society before we can develop a universal philosophy encompassing—and morally solving—all social, economic and political world problems. Many problems presently facing us must be solved in the light of collective Truth, sharing in cooperative efforts of Universal Consciousness.

Individuals living a predominantly physical life feel safer in retaining old, comfortable living patterns. To investigate unknown territory takes courage. Many times old habits are reluctant to die in order to acquire a new cloak of light. Being new, it may not fit as comfortably as the old cloak of familiar habitual thought.

The rebirthing itself is an experience that can shake one to the core.

It is also disarming to the conscious mind to be thrust into new paths of expressions, yet, if one is to fulfill his or her destiny, a willingness must persist to shake old habits, and reach up for the stars now within their orbit.

The true seeker of light keeps asking for greater and greater Truth, and has the courage to examine the Truth, for the Master Jesus has said, "He who asks shall receive." He was speaking of spiritual as well as emotional and physical needs.

If one is fearful of Truth received, then reluctance to expand consciousness into deeper spiritual realms results. Therefore, one must not ask if not willing to examine what is received. Understanding can be challenging because of the multiple human expressions of God. One must be freed from shades of training imposed by limited insights. This demands discernment and discrimination of knowledge received.

Accentuated growth also brings into one's consciousness, an awareness of the greater plan unfolding on the plane of spirit.

The enlightened individual begins to perceive a glimmer of the great plan of God as the veil is slowly disintegrating before his or her eyes.

For a very few, the plan is unfolded in one master stroke to astound the mind. Yet, the enlightened one still accepts instantaneous Truth because the soul has been readied for this sudden illumination. For others, it comes more slowly, depending on prior preparation to receive enlightenment.

When the student is ready, the inner master will appear. The truth "as above, so below" begins to penetrate the enlightened consciousness.

One finally finds design and order, and consciously sees the rule of law in operation both in the letter and the spirit. It becomes more familiar. One discovers the need for law, the necessity of order. One recognizes the mathematics of the law of organized living and applies the law of unconditional love daily.

But the enlightened individual has said, "From whence comes the law?"

Divine law, as they remembered it from the beginning, functioned in a pattern that balanced the spiritual energies in perfect symmetry. The pattern of balance must be imprinted upon dense matter. It has taken many incarnations before the pattern unfolded in humanity's recall.

Limited understanding of the law does not keep it from operating. The Master Plan has been unfolding all along.

Knowing that the law continues to function beyond present comprehension, giving security and trust in inner God awareness, one now worships with a new understanding. One knows that the limits of finite understanding is not the totality of Truth.

This awareness keeps one from becoming dogmatic, permitting an open mind toward the observations of others, giving ability and freedom to listen to revelations of others that might enlighten understanding. One finally recognizes that fellow beings, at their level of enlightenment, are interpreting the law as they understand and perceive it.

One no longer feels a need to argue or defend one's position, secure in the knowledge of being loved for oneself and feeling a revered Light of God. Grounded in universal love, one no longer feels threatened by having personal limitations examined, even abandoned, to the Truth now being exposed.

The enlightened one can now see spiritual laws operating on the earth plane, delegated authority existing on all levels. One begins to see the structure of delegated authority "as above so below." There must be assigned responsibilities, depending upon the depth of awareness of new spiritual law, and more importantly, willingness to accept one's duty for making this law operate.

This has brought forth the Hierarchical chain of command, according to willingness to abide by it.

Being spiritually oriented, humanity could comprehend that authority had to be delegated, had to operate for the benefit of the weak and the strong, equally. Much injustice has been done by a limited understanding of the law. Abuse of power does not invalidate the fact that authority must exist and is functional.

The old law that ruled upon the Earth, "An eye for an eye and a tooth for a tooth," has brought injustice and misunderstanding among humanity, but at least the law was recognized, no matter how stringent.

The enlightenment of the true law as given by the Master Jesus gave man hope and release not known previously for centuries. To love God, and one's neighbor as oneself, was a revelation comprehended by very few, and is still not applied even 2,000 years later.

Cycles

Master Jesus said, "I come to bring the Truth, and the Truth shall set you free."

Do you think we are ready for a new revelation? One of the tasks of the Aquarian Age is to awaken people to an awareness of their own essential divinity, and to bring a measure of unity between the churches, as well as tolerance for one another.

Another goal is to bring the best of religion to the attention of the scientists. Science is beginning to penetrate the world of intangibles, essences, and origins through parapsychology and higher mind investigation. Humanity will eventually acknowledge the existence of the etheric level of existence. So the Aquarian dispensation has to be a scientific age. It has to be a spiritual scientific age that is going to win, save, inspire, and guide.

Every created thing has its cycle of fulfillment, and every Dispensation has its era, then evolves into the next. If any major planetary event occurs in the world at this time, there will be change, and the Piscean cycle comes to an end.

So this is the most important aspect—that "we make a new beginning" and encourage those sympathetic to universality to start our studies anew.

After individuals have acquainted themselves with the overall vision of the ageless Wisdom Teachings, they are ready for a more profound esoteric nature. There has to be a new beginning.

We Are In Transition

In the latter part of the Twentieth Century, we began the transitional period between two Dispensations—the ending of the old Piscean doctrine, yet not quite ready for the energies of the new Aquarian Dispensation.

This is why the present age partakes of both the old and new—a clinging to tradition, yet yearning for greater enlightenment through a period of religious transition, a literal and symbolic pre-dawning.

This accounts also—to a large degree—for the chaotic thinking which seems to have replaced the steadfast faith held by our predecessors. We are sheep listening for the sound of the shepherd's voice.

The revelation of Jesus the Christ, as given to John, states in Revelations Chapter 20 that there is to be an extended period of peace coming to Earth. This period was to commence around the end of the 20th Century.

Now, in our time, after 2,000 years, comes the fulfillment of the prophecy, "Out of Egypt will I call my Suns."

From out of the ancient Coptic Temple has come the teaching of the Coptic Fellowship of America, the 20th Century Masters who have, through the ages, carried in their minds and hearts the Truth which is now unfolding, the mysteries so long protected by the Masters of the Coptic heritage—once known as the Essene Order, the White Brotherhood—tracing back to Atlantis.

When the 49th state—Alaska—was added to the U.S., that signified the beginning, the actual beginning of the New Dispensation, which was the fulfillment of the first states of life's purpose—objective purpose—of the United States and the beginning of the age of a new era.

Karma

It is of no consequence to the world whether or not an individual accepts theological doctrine, or that the Gospel story is accepted in detail.   If an individual wants to concentrate his or her energies on interpretations of who and what God is, who or what the Christ is, that is entirely one's prerogative.

What is of ultimate importance is whether people have love in their hearts for God, for their neighbors, and for themselves as sparks of divinity. This is the true measure of individual redemption.

For human enlightenment, we shall concentrate on delegation of authority and operation of law as it affects the Earth.

All manifestation of energy occurs first in spirit. When persons can comprehend this concept, they will be able to encompass the law that will bring peace and justice to all the operations of Earth beings.

Hierarchy sets up the master plan for this particular planet and other planets. The next in command attends to seeing it carried forth on different levels until it filters into the consciousness of humanity, which has had the veil drawn upon the knowledge that they are an original spark of God.

Individuals must use free will to develop their own individuality that shall eventually commune with the Central Source. By then, personal vibrations shall be extremely high. They will have highly developed spiritual bodies, much lighter than their present physical bodies.

Seven Decrees of the New Law

One of the great signs of the New Order has been given to the earth plane by the Hierarchy. It is a new dispensation —a NEW LAW to replace the old dispensation of Moses and the Ten Commandments. THE LAW OF THE ONLY ONE has been given in SEVEN DECREES:

FIRST DECREE

Thou shall not adulterate the law within your own being. Be in spirit with that which is Love of self. Love that which created you and of like beings for all is all.

SECOND DECREE

Behold your mother and your father as the giver of Light. Walk not in mistrust of yourself and others. Be guided only from that wisdom with you.

THIRD DECREE

Other houses have I. You shall not invade the abode of others, for this is their sacred birthright.

FOURTH DECREE

Behold the Lightbearers. Their light is from one source, but of different gleamings. Together the Light shall be whole.

FIFTH DECREE

Fret not over your awakening. All shall come according to inward command. Patience shall be upon your brow and in your heart.

SIXTH DECREE

Behold I come lightly and in good time. Darkness shall never invade your path as you seek the Light.

SEVENTH DECREE

All wisdom and all knowledge is within. Seek no other sources lest they be false teachings. I have spoken and you shall obey and know ME.

Creating Positive Karma

While developing the qualities of World Light energy as an inward, individual happening, the outward expression of the group mind occurs in small and large groups.

Altruistic service and sharing is an essential part of the unfolding and manifestation of the responsibility that World Light demands.

World Light has always been perpetuated these millions of years on the Earth. It is in the original cells of memory, the blood streams, and the sinews of humanity to fellowship with one another. There is a basic need that goes much deeper than man and woman coming together to co-habit and bring forth offspring. It is a deep spiritual need, a calling to each other's souls to come together to enrich individual lives, to share, to grow in spirit and wisdom together.

Though a person must go into his private sanctuary before his own altar, one must then go forth and openly share wisdom gained from the silence of one's private communion. This ultimate sharing has always existed. Society has been fractured and splintered, yet even in its splintering, people have always gathered together to soothe their mental and emotional wounds and nurture one another perennially toward higher awareness.

Humankind has come to a definite fork in the road on the earth plane once again. The choice is ours: shall we continue to emphasize our differences or shall we finally begin to look past appearances, and build a mighty foundation upon our common attributes and common heritage?

You, The Reader

The preparation for the return of universality upon the Earth has been underway for the past 50 years. Whether an individual soul shall see God as a part of oneself is a personal determination each one must make. This determination is made within the heart and soul of every man, woman, and child on the earth plane.

Humanity must rid itself of a belief in negativity and its companion, fear, if we are ever to realize our dream of peace. Fear is the bane of civilization. It breeds intolerance, adversity, and separatism. It closes our minds to the Truth, and blinds us to a greater reality. And the only way we will conquer our fear is to examine its source openly.

Casting fear aside is only the first step, however. In order for us, as a species, to continue to grow and evolve, we must band together and pool our collective resources—physical, financial, and spiritual—to solve the world problems.

We must come to regard ourselves as one people. We can no longer afford an "Us versus Them" approach to international relationships. This way of thinking has been the source of the degradation of the environment, the oppression of people, overpopulation, and the obvious—war. With the return of the Christ within each of us, that energy will transport us to a greater reality where all will live in cooperation and harmony. We are all potential avatars. We all carry within us the stuff of which Messiahs are made.

If you are reading this book, you are part of this group, whether conscious of it or not. The fact that you were drawn to its message is evidence enough. One need not be conscious of his/her mission to be able to fulfill it on the physical plane.

There are many servers who would scoff at the idea that they are carrying out a plan devised by an unseen spiritual board of directors designed to help the planet transition to its next level on its evolutionary journey. Even so, this does not diminish the contribution they make. And in truth, knowledge of one's part in the plan is only a secondary consideration. Carrying it out is the primary goal.

Human Affairs Inseparable from Spiritual Reality

People are realizing that the state of human affairs cannot be separated from spiritual reality, and more importantly, that they cannot leave it "up to God." We must stop being spectators and become initiators for action.

It is our responsibility to reverse the negativity and damage that has been done to our planet and our species for we have created it. Groups that are wishing and waiting for some extraterrestrial civilization to appear in their spaceships and save us from destruction—or expecting to be "raptured" to heaven—fail to realize this. It is up to us. And we must do it now. Jesus said it nearly 2,000 years ago. "Now is the appointed time."

People need to talk about commonality rather than differences and boundaries. If spiritually oriented people became committed to the principle of unity and universal love, it would change the world.

Humanity must have the courage and will to educate its youth to respect that the right human relations are vital to a peaceful world, and then to give them the opportunity to pursue them.

The United States should be poised to begin this process. It is part of the heritage of America to promote the ideals of freedom and choice. This heritage goes to the heart and soul of America, and was imprinted upon its spirit at the time of its founding by an illumined group of people who recognized the integral part that spirituality plays in human life. They intended this spirit to serve as the ideal to which other nations could aspire.

Creating the World You Want

The birth of the universal consciousness within one's own being is the most powerful happening that can occur within the individual. This is the crowning achievement, the first movement toward the complete oneness, the connection between the individualized spark and the Godhead. This is the total link between God and humanity.

A simple daily regimen of meditation, prayer, and practical action in whatever form suits you—volunteerism, environmental activism, or other humanitarian endeavor—is all that is required to create the world you want. It does require discipline and the willingness to encourage others to do the same, for manifestation works best when the participants are great in number.

This is the calling, which the World Server hears. Every person on the planet who responds to the inner desire to serve in some fashion is a part of this group of world servers, and the contribution of each is as significant as that of the collective.

The authority figure within us (WILL) is what we are attempting to awaken into daily successful habits. The word 'will' means 'light.'

Those authority figures that we criticize subconsciously remind us what we are attempting to master in this life.

212

It is amazing how wise our birth father and mother become as we get older. Our birth father, symbolizing Will, and our birth mother, symbolizing Love, represent our earliest childhood recollections of the mirror of the personal Will and Love within us that manifest later in our life. What we have to face in life, is what our father and mother symbolically expressed to us when we were children. "Out of a little acorn (childhood), grows a great oak tree (adulthood)."

Overcome what our birth father and mother couldn't, and embrace positively what they were in our own unique way, and we manifest in our daily lives the important lessons of Will and Love. When we learn to forgive our birth father and mother, and forgive their weaknesses, and thank them for what they taught us in a positive way, we achieve the Judas forgiveness goals of the magnificent Easter seasons—"Forgive him, Father, he knows not what he does."

The term Light of the World refers to the pure consciousness of the spirit, and is a title given to one who has completely overcome all temptations, all attachments which pertain to the material life, and lives in the field of complete inspiration. They feel the pain of others, and are ever seeking to alleviate that pain, thereby giving expression to the great light.

This is the task that you, the reader, must strive to achieve, however impossible it may at first appear.

What follows are some suggestions on how you may approach this monumental task.

Maintaining a Positive Focus

As we begin to understand the deeper reality of thoughts and the way our minds function, we can learn to become master of our mind, and truly to become the leader of our evolution, as well as make it the key to unlocking our higher potential.

ACCEPT that you are here to grow and evolve. Life doesn't always go smoothly. Not everything is meant to be a joyride or an exercise in pleasure. Life's lessons can be difficult, but are more so if you approach them with avoidance and apprehension. If you see them as opportunities to become stronger, wiser, and more resilient, you are thinking positively and productively.

Attitude is a mindset. It is the way you look at things mentally. A positive attitude is the outward manifestation of a mind that dwells primarily on positive matters.

I think of what Gloria Moorehead taught us at the S.U.N. Conference when she spoke on "Be the change you are looking for" In other words, if you want to be a positive person and get positive results, you have to OWN IT, THINK IT, BE IT. What you think, you become. THOUGHTS ARE THINGS.

You Are Not Limited

You are not limited to the life you now live. It has been accepted by you as the best you can do at this moment. Any time you're ready to go beyond the limitations currently in your life, you're capable of doing that by choosing positive thoughts. All you must do is figure out how you can do it— not whether you can. And once you have made up your mind to do it, it's amazing how your mind begins to figure out how.

The key to success is to influence the subconscious mind and set up new habits and behavior. The subconscious responds to repetition. Repeating a positive affirmation to yourself will make it respond. Try saying something like,

"Every day, in every way, things are getting better and better."

Making and affirming your own personal declaration will make a world of difference in your outlook and your habits. Design your own upbeat daily declarations and deliver them to yourself in the mirror. Some ideas are: I am love, I am joy, I am might, I am strength, I am peace, I am glory.

The subconscious is always receptive to suggestions that transpire from your conscious mind, so keep your conscious mind filled with creative, positive, pleasant, peaceful, and productive thoughts. When you repeat an affirmation in a relaxed state of mind, it works even better. To retain these suggestions, repeat them often till you feel confident that they have become a permanent habit.

Wake up every morning and say I'm love, I'm joy, I'm peace, I'm strength, I'm might, I'm power, I'm happy, and I'm healthy. You just empowered yourself. It's called reprogramming. We have to love ourselves enough to reprogram our thinking.

In addition, you can train the emotions into responding favorably. When we smile, it releases chemicals in the brain that make us feel good. Try looking in the mirror and grinning at yourself. Don't feel self-conscious—just do it. You will be amazed at how good it makes you feel. Also, make sure you SMILE when you meet people. It will make you feel good and they will respond to you. Turn yourself into a SMILE MILLIONAIRE!

These Words Can Create Positive Conditions

WE CAN – Everything depends on your attitude of mind. We CAN if we think we CAN.

WE WILL – "We will" is positive and shows determination to follow through on that which we think is right for us to do.

EXPECT THE BEST – Expect the best, and we will get the best because we have the right attitude of mind. This mysterious formula works. Make it work for our collective good.

WE KNOW – When saying "We know" it means there is no doubt in our mind, for our inner being is stepping forth in a positive manner. We have acquired the facts to fortify our knowing.

WE WILL FIND TIME – No matter how busy we are, we can always find time to be helpful to others in need of help, if we think in a straight line—positively.

POSITIVITY – This indicates a burning desire which brings forth positive results.

WE ARE CONFIDENT – By replacing ignorance with knowledge and wisdom, the end product will be self-confidence.

WE BELIEVE – These words symbolize positivity on all three planes—the physical, the mental, and the spiritual. It would be wise to carry this formula with us and every time we feel ourselves slipping into the field of "We can't" to read it so as to reset our mind.

If we do this, we will be surprised at the great planetary change which will take place on the planet. It will affect both our own mental attitude and that of other people because we will be projecting what is going on in our mind into the minds of other people, and they, in turn, create positive thoughts for the future of planet Earth.

The snowball effect this will have on the planet will be amazing! Radical positive changes in a very short period of time are not only possible, but inevitable! We can do this if we work together. Your help is needed, and right now!

Our collective goal is a positive planetary resurrection.

Conviction Is Key

The mind must be made like a clear, blank, white screen.   Only the idea you wish to accomplish should appear there—nothing else. Focus your thoughts upon the idea, thus strengthening it. See that the idea is completely molded, but do not think with intensity about your idea all day long. Neither should the intensity of relaxation be all day long. There is a time to think, and a time to relax.

If you are overly emotional, get control over of your emotions, and realize that your mind has stabilized itself because you now have at your disposal many units of energy. Your brain is only one small part of you, for you have billions of cells in your physical body.

Therefore, before you can fulfill an idea which your brain has projected, you have to convince every cell of your physical body—every cell of your physical body must be coordinated in harmony of action. If you decide to start meditating and exercising regularly, you start to do so, and then your body says, "I am too tired. I want to sit and rest." This is because you have not convinced your resisting body that it should cooperate. So you need to concentrate more, and create a rhythm until your body cooperates with you, because you are the master of your body.

When the idea you are concentrating upon becomes part of you, it will be accepted by your subconscious mind. Then it will become a blueprint of what you wish.

Your physical body and your mind will move with the purpose of that blueprint and every person who comes in contact with you will feel that purpose. Thus you become an astral salesman because you are projecting your idea so positively that you convince people to the extent that they cooperate in helping bring your idea to fulfillment.

This is because the conviction you yourself have concerning your idea becomes the conviction also of others, thereby building up a FAITH which results in the fulfillment of your idea. However this faith in yourself needs a sustaining power—the power of God. So there is another formula which should be kept in mind and practiced.

We're going to pray because that is so powerful. We focus on the goal and it's all positive.

A Daily Spiritual World Unity Love and Light Projection

I put my Family in a pyramid of light and love.

I put my City in a pyramid of light and love.

I put my State in a pyramid of light and love.

I put my Country in a pyramid of light and love.

I put the North American continent in a pyramid of light and love.

I put the South American continent in a pyramid of light and love.

I put the Asian continent in a pyramid of light and love.

I put the European continent in a pyramid of light and love.

I put the African continent in a pyramid of light and love.

I put the Australian continent in a pyramid of light and love.

I put the Polar Regions in a pyramid of light and love.

I put all other lands and peoples in a pyramid of light and love.

I put all other planes of existence in a pyramid of light and love.

I put all other planets and galaxies in a pyramid of light and love.

Guideposts to Becoming a Light of the World

Listed below are several guideposts to becoming a light of the world.

Keep these thoughts in mind at all times, and the effect they have on you, the people around you, and the world at large will be nothing short of a miracle.

YOU ARE A MIGHTY, POWERFUL, SPIRITUAL BEING

BELIEVE IN YOURSELF – You weren't an accident. You weren't mass produced. You aren't an assembly line product. You were deliberately planned, specifically gifted, and lovingly positioned on the Earth by the Master craftsman.

BELIEVING IN YOURSELF IS AN ATTITUDE AND A CHOICE – It takes a positive attitude.

THE CHOICE OF WHAT TO BELIEVE IS UP TO YOU – You have to give up "I can't." Don't waste your life believing you can't, because with God, all things are possible.

IT'S ALL ABOUT ATTITUDE – What others think about you is none of your business. You have to believe in yourself when no one else does. That's what makes you a winner. You operate as if everyone is a part of a plot to enhance your well-being.

WHEN LIFE HANDS YOU A LEMON, SQUEEZE IT AND MAKE LEMONADE – Look for the opportunity in everything.

IF SOMETHING NEGATIVE HAPPENS TO YOU, REMEMBER GOD HAS SOMETHING MORE IN STORE FOR YOU.

USE THE POWER OF GOAL SETTING – If you want to be happy, set a goal that commands your thoughts, liberates your energy, and inspires your hopes.

WRITE OUT YOUR GOALS SOON AND THEN VERBALLY REPEAT THESE GOALS

CREATE A GOALS BOOK AND CARRY YOUR MOST IMPORTANT GOAL IN YOUR WALLET – Reread your goals three times a day for the next three days. You need goals that stretch you.

MASTERY IS THE GOAL – You want to set a goal that is big enough that in the process of achieving, you increase your self-respect.

DO IT NOW!

Thinking Big, the Key to Your Destiny

I have some news for you. There's suppose to be a return of the world teacher—a new Messiah—and I've got the name! I'm going to give it to you now. First name? Thin. Last name? King. Thin-King. Thinking! That's what we've got to bring to this new age.

The great ones (such as the round table) lived so we could emulate them. Jesus said, "Greater things than I do ye shall do." And guess what? We have an opportunity to do this. This is the age of Aquarius! It's right now! We are here to think so big it's unbelievable. It's all about everyone. All this energy is so important to the planet. And you are a carrier of this dynamic energy.

This age is full of positivity—love, and light.

The new age is truly at this level, the pineal gland. The symbol of the pineal gland is 666. Taking responsibility for the physical, mental, emotional, and spiritual. That's what 666 means. That's what we're here to do. Take responsibility. This responsibility is what we're here to learn. To learn to think bigger than we've ever thought before.

Because Aquarius is an air age—and when you reach an air age, you're attracted to it. From the other side, you found out the Earth was going through a transformation. You raised your hand. Because you know you had that positive thinking. You've had many, many lifetimes here. When you move into an air age, we become co-creators. That's what you wanted to do. You loved this earth plane so much you went back to the school of the Earth.

The Utilization of Atomic Energy for Altruistic Planetary Service

From my understanding, the use of positive atomic energy is now being made available to those individuals and groups who understand the nature and structure of its laws.

One of the many uses of the atom is in the power of personal and group prayer and planetary thought projection. Let us first differentiate between the important difference between the Earth (body) an the world (mind). The physical Earth success is directly attributed to the proper use of individual and collective minds in everyday usage. What we see on Earth is directly related to how we are using our minds int he realization of our goals and dreams in our families and jobs. Project this simple individual meaning into a mass consciousness of 6.5 billion souls, and you can visualize a huge mass-mind computer directly impacting our humanity daily.

In the year 2012, we were asked as individuals "who knew that we knew" to start using this powerful atomic theory to change the world computer—the mind of the earth plane.

On an individual mind level, the atom is comprised of the proton (a positive polarity representing our conscious mind), the electron (a passive polarity representing our subconscious mind), and the neutron (a neutral energy representing our superconscious mind).

We inadvertently use these powers of the atom every day of our lives without realizing we are actually employing the atomic theory in going abut the process of living our normal lives. What most of us don't realize is that we are able to expand the use of the atom on a much broader scale, impacting man planes of mental consciousness simultaneously.

To use the power of the atom on a broad all-encompassing scale, the law of the atom speaks very clearly. We can only use the power of the atom on a positive, constructive level. The power of the atom is to be used for healing any situation on a physical, mental, or etheric level. If the motive for the use of atomic theory is for a selfish or destructive purpose, the process kicks into a self-protective level, and the atomic power immediately "kicks off" and is inoperable. This theory is to be compared to a circuit breaker in our home. When too much electrical power is used at one time in our house, the circuit breaker "kicks in" and the power goes off.

Just think of the magnificent use of the atomic theory as we as individuals and groups send positive and constructive energy in the mental ethers to impact our society on a world (collective mind) level.

Let us start calling on the use of atomic mental power to bring forth our dreams of manifestation for a greater Earth on all levels of our world society.

Here are some simple ideas to be enacted during your quiet moments of contemplation every day. Prior to your meditation or prayer session, call upon the power of the atom to be with you during your time of thought projection. Remember your motive is for the benefit of others. The purer the personal motive—the more powerful is the atomic energy.

Steps to call upon the power of the atom:

1. Send thoughts of healing to those you know who are ailing.
2. Send thoughts of love and peace to people who live on all seven continents in a bubble of light.

(A bubble can be the size of a molecule or a solar system.)

3. Send thoughts of instruction impacting our Earth leaders sitting in a roundtable. Ask in your own words that the vision of world peace, world unity, and world sharing be made a permanent part of their government agenda.

Maybe your personal prayer might be that a choice offered to those suffering on our Earth be given the choice of a place to live or that the starving on the Earth be sent food from those countries who have an abundance of food reserves.

When enough of us are properly using the great power of the atom in our thought projections daily, we will see an ongoing positive transformation not experienced before on the earth plane. Only because we took a few minutes every day to mentally create for our earth brothers and sisters the proper mental environment for their hopes and dreams to become a reality. To maintain the selfless purity of our individual motive, this altruistic technique is for the benefit of everyone except us.

You Are the Light of the World

We need to plant the seeds—remember.

As a planetary numerologist, I realized that certain important dates translate to "the Light of the World." The Light of the World was the first day of the Mayan calendar, as well as December 21, 2012. Some people thought the world would end—remember that? The energy contained in this phrase is the most positive energy I've ever experienced as a planetary numerologist.

The same energy came up again in the years 2013, 2014, and 2015! January 1st, 2017 marks the beginning of a new 9-year cycle, one in which significant changes can be made by the Light of the World.

Guess who is the Light of the World? Sitting in your chair! That's how powerful you are. Remember you are the light of the world. Pray for the benefit of all nations and peoples.

Our job is to master our desires on the earth plane. Every day is a conception day. In 9 months, or 9 years, or 90 years, your daily prayers are going to manifest.

Every day is a potential springtime day for each of us to accept our responsibility as a co-creator. What do you do in the springtime? You plant seeds. We are the world servers.

We were talked about Alice Bailey back around 1900 and she said that all world servers would be born and activated into world service around the year 2000. And guess what? That happened! World peace, world unity, world sharing, world prosperity. All the hungry find food, the homeless find homes. And remember, politicians, the women are equal to men. Empower those women! This is the feminine millennium. That was a conception. So this conception day—the seeds are going to grow. War will be abolished by all governments. The only place they'll resolve their issues is at the negotiating table.

Pray For Your Country

What do you want for your country? A greater economy? All the things that are happening in the country —you want them better? Say them every day. Pray for the country. Every day. We don't know what the challenges are, so we pray every day, every day, every day.

225

The U.S. of A. is going through a springtime, and we, living in the greatest country in the world, are the ones who get this information, are going to be the ones who transform this country.

When we incarnate again we'll say, "What happened in 2015 to 2025? What happened to this planet?" And you were the ones to plant the seeds to create it. And by the way, we don't remember our past lifetimes because we'd just be reliving them all the time. We're living all those lifetimes at the same time anyway. This is the life. We're living our past lifetimes all at the same time.

Think of it. In your hands, with all dealings, with financial security and financial prosperity, for us, our country, and all countries. It's just so powerful. I'm just so excited about this! And now you know. And by the way, this information isn't copyrighted. I want you to share this with as many people as possible.

What a responsibility! Pure heart. Pure heart. That's where we are. Pure heart. To manifest positivity and love and light for this planet. All we have to do is be a Light of the World.

The Traveler's Creed

We walk the middle path, the path toward light. We follow no human, and no human shall follow us. It is a road that we must go alone, and we are valiant and brave for the journey. We are a fragment of divinity returning to the whole from which we sprang, and within us is the power to know and to choose the steps we must take.

We are the sister and brother of all men and women, and honor the freedom that is ours. We walk with humankind and cherish only love for our fellow beings, believing and knowing that each in their own time must work out their triumphant destiny.

A Declaration for a United Humanity

WE, as members of humanity, recognize a potential on Planet Earth for a just Peace and Unity, a balance of health and abundance for all.   This inspires us to know our Oneness and impels us to action, action to manifest a United Humanity. We pledge our lives and dedicate ourselves to these basic truths:

WE AFFIRM there is Unity in the life force within all that is. This Unity includes all names and forms. All life forms are unique expressions of this Unity.

WE RECOGNIZE the place of each individual and Planet Earth in the unfolding Universe. To express this reality, we respect all life, and we share life's abundance. We support opportunities for self-fulfillment, and freedom of expression for all.

WE RESOLVE AND DEDICATE ourselves to be an expression of unity at all times and in all places. Our Unity calls us to serve with love, compassion, and understanding. Our oneness creates trust, harmony, and peace, and reflects the very nature of our being.

WE ACT for World Unity in the practice of these basic truths.

May God's Blessings Be With Us

So with that, I leave you with this . . .

Be ever so mindful of the thoughts you entertain. They have the power to become your reality. For they steer you to a greater or lesser degree, in the direction of your life. The more focused the thought, the more definite the result. We move in the direction of our faith. Energy moves in the direction of thought.   And remember, every morning you awaken . . . take a good look in the mirror . . .smile . . .and with a genuine feeling of gratitude and appreciation, say "I love you." And mean it!

We should all meditate and pray daily for the full embodiment of God's plan on Earth—the return of the universal oneness through the Light of the World.

May hope, joy, support, and blessing of all God's creation and kingdoms be with us this moment as we participate in the Mass of Universality, the festival of our true identity—Divinity with humility.